Jane Stern

Trucker

A Portrait of the last American Cowboy

McGraw-Hill
Book Company

New York
St. Louis
San Francisco
Dusseldorf
London
Mexico
Sydney
Toronto

456789   RABP   78976

Library of Congress Cataloging in Publication Data

Stern, Jane.
      Trucker: a portrait of the last American cowboy.

      1. Motor-truck drivers—United States.
I. Title.
HD8039.T72U47   301.44'42   75-6885
ISBN 0-07-061201-3
ISBN 0-07-061202-1 pbk.

Book design by A Good Thing, Inc.

Original photographs by Jane and Michael Stern

To Michael

Preface

A book about truckdrivers does not get written by a non-trucker without help from those who know the roads. For three years I chronicled the life of those men and women who run the long hauls, focusing on the wildcatters and truckers whose rigs are their only homes. I rode with more than I can remember and, when I wasn't inside a truck, I was driving fast behind one in my yellow car loaded with cameras, tape cassettes, my husband Michael, who served as co-photographer, and a toothless bulldog named Richard.

I was first excited by the nomadic and romantic trucker's life through the country-western songs of men like Red Simpson and Dick Curless, whose lyrics detail the gearjammers legends and customs. I responded to the music as myth until I met my first truckdriver face to face, and the legend turned to fact. I realized then that the myths of the open road were expressed not only in the songs, but in poetry and in the day-to-day life of many a trucker.

But it's been a long haul between that inspiration and this book. I would like to extend my thanks to those who have helped along the way: Kathy Matthews, my editor, provided patience, an educated judgment, and the friendship that saw this book to completion. My husband Michael acted beyond the call of his duty as photographer, chauffeur, bodyguard, typist, and friend. His evenings at home were often interrupted by anonymous gearjammers parading through his living room, or seated across from him at the dinner table. I am especially grateful to Julia Welch, Susanna Rodell, Theodore Willentz, and Fred Hills for their part in making *Trucker* a reality. Special thanks also to M. J. Burnet, Howard Merk, Jr., and Gene Murphy for their long-standing open-door policies at their truck stops. I am grateful to the Peterbilt Company, especially Jack Lounsbury, and to the Kenworth Company and Bob Dayharsh; to truckdrivers John Laney, Jack Hamilton, Jean Sawyer, Bill Couchenour, Joe West, and Jim Hearty for their interest and their patience with my ignorance of the mechanics of trucking; and to Paul Kirouac, for his enthusiasm and appreciation for the subject; to Florence and Harry Stern for their hospitality and generous help; to Norma and Teddy Doob, for their love and encouragement; and to Ellen and David James, for surviving Naked City. Most of all, I thank the hundreds of truckdrivers whose names I never learned, but whose encouragement and friendship I'll never forget.

All of the poems in this book, unless otherwise specified, are the work of truckdriver Jack Hamilton.

Contents

Introduction

The time is 1875. The town is old El Paso. The sun glitters off the fine particles of dust kicked up by the hooves of the cowboy's horse. He's almost home. Three weeks on the trail, and just fifty miles to go before he can kick off his boots in front of his own hearthstone. His bones are smarting from fatigue, and his bandanna is tied low around his face to protect his mouth from gritty road dirt. He has driven a load of cattle to that little town far down the trail, and now, with his pocket full of silver dollars, he is heading for the nearest saloon for a bath and a shave and maybe a woman. His horse's coat is covered with a frothy sweat despite the heavy Navaho saddle blankets and the bitter winter weather. Clouds of steam jet forth from the horse's dilated nostrils. As he approaches the Diamond L saloon, the cowboy dismounts and wraps the horse's reins, studded with silver conches, around a wooden post. Rump to rump with other quarter horses, the horse tugs at the bridle and stomps the earth as the air is filled with the sound of labored breathing. Rubbing the grit from his eyes, the cowboy surveys the scene momentarily and pushes through the swinging wooden door, heading for a shot of whiskey and some companionship.

The time is now 1975. The town is El Paso. The long-haul trucker is pulling into the Diamond L truck stop. He has driven practically coast-to-coast in three days, and he hasn't seen his family in more than four weeks. His face is prematurely lined with creases that deepen with the brutal hours of life on the open road. His stomach is rebelling at the diet of greasy pork chops and endless coffee wolfed down in a blurred chain of truck stops.

The radiator grill of his truck is muffled against the cold with heavy, quilted blankets and, as he eases it into the long line of parked trucks, its throaty idle joins the chorus of other giant engines. The trucker has just picked up $800 for dropping off a load of cattle in some distant town. Once inside the truck stop, he will head for the barber shop, the laundry room, and the gift shop for a shave, a wash, and a pile of souvenirs for his wife and kids. But more than refreshment or trinkets, he wants the comradeship offered by the other truck-drivers—men who, like himself, are a long way from home and will help him to forget his loneliness for a time. The trucker climbs down the metal steps of his cab and onto the concrete apron of the truck stop, his cowboy boot narrowly missing a puddle of spilled engine oil. He quickly admires the shiny silver hood ornament on the nose of a new Diamond Reo parked next to his old Thermodyne, and slowly, his legs cramped from the long haul, he heads through the swinging doors marked "professional drivers only" for a cup of coffee and some companionship.

Passing through the doors of any truck stop, be it a modern, formica-and-glass auto-truck complex or a back road Ma-and-Pa diner, you will still see plenty to remind you of the Old West. Of course there are evolutionary changes. The modern truckdriver would hardly wear spurs or chaps while driving, but at the counter of any truck stop you will still see the men wearing western hats, silver-tipped cowboy boots, and snap-button frontier shirts. In addition to the wardrobe that echoes the Old West, you will see the slow, rolling gait that is associated with men who spend more time riding horses than pounding pavement. You won't see bowlegs on many trucker-cowboys, but you will notice that slight hesitation as if the adjustment from sitting to walking doesn't come easy. The old-timers still carry a pouch of Bull Durham tobacco, and even if they don't chew, it comes in handy, when rubbed on the windshield, to keep the rain from beading.

As he enters the diner, the trucker steps into a world of instant friends—but friends who keep their distance. Around the turn of the century, a cowboy named Andy

Downs said, "The West demands you smile and swallow your personal troubles like your food. Nobody wants to listen to another man's half-digested problems." Among the truckers, there is a feeling of shared experience in a muted, insulated atmosphere. Eyes seldom meet, and elbows are kept close to the body. In conversation, only certain topics are safe because they're not intrusive. You can talk about your truck, the weather, the food, the road, anything mechanical, and women—as long as it's not your wife. You can ask a trucker where he's headed, or ask him whom he hauls for, but you wouldn't ask what's in the trailer any more than you'd ask a cowboy what's in his saddle bags. That's his business, and whether the load is legal or not, valuable or worthless, it's his personal and private responsibility.

Even the most road-weary gearjammer is always ready to talk about his truck. Prod him with a few questions, and once he gets the initial complaining out of the way, a smile will spread over his face and he will tell you about his current favorite and all the other trucks he has ever driven. There are trucks that are as slow and heavy as Clydesdale horses. They are designed to pull the heaviest loads over great distances. There are lighter trucks, designed for speed and agility, carrying loads around mountain bends with the sure-footedness of a pinto pony. Some trucks purr. Others growl. The sound of a releasing air brake is similar to the sound of air exploding from an appaloosa stud's nostrils. Nothing is as thrilling to a trucker as the grand scale of his rig. The high-up cowhide seat, like the saddle of a horse, gives a majestic perspective on the world. Most trucks, like most horses, aren't really legend material. But many do become legends if only in the minds of their owners. It wasn't uncommon for cowboys to construct gravestones for their horses.

Jim
a reel hors
oct 1, 82

And often, after two million miles of reliable service, a trucker might decide to keep the hood ornament of the truck that served him so well.

Curtness of speech and manner was a western characteristic. The constant loneliness of the prairie condensed speech to a few well-chosen words, which were all the more colorful for their requisite compactness. In designing a sentence, a cowboy would "bobtail her

4

and fill her with meat." The cowboy's pistol was a "blue whistler" and its bullet a "lead plum." Likewise, a trucker rides in his "bucket of bolts," listening to the "hillbilly opera house," and stopping at his favorite "choke-and-puke" for a cup of "mud."

Every trucker feels his truck has a definite and distinct personality and, like the cowboy's horse, it is probably nicknamed. If he drives for a large fleet, it might be "Old 85" or "Miss 201" or "Phantom 509." If the truck is his own, the name will be more intimately evocative: "Sherman's Tank," "French Fry Express," "Tennessee Mack," "Dirty-Minded Diesel," or just plain "Stacked." Some might be named after wives or girl friends, but it's a truckers' superstition that one named after an ex-wife can only bring doom to it's driver. The names can usually be found hand-lettered on the front of the cab in a fancy script and elaborate design that's probably the best graffiti on wheels.

With the growing popularity of the Citizen's Band radio among truckers, every gearjammer on Channel 10 has to have his own unique handle. "Cheyenne Wrangler," "The Denver Kid," and "Texas Tumbleweed" are all riding the airwaves today. Even before the CB radio, truckers, like cowboys, sported names descriptive of unique physical characteristics: "Sleepy," "Skinny," "Red," "Pop," or "Shorty."

It isn't unusual to hear one trucker call another "cowboy." Usually a sarcastic handle, "cowboy" refers to a driver who is reckless or spends all his money on fancy boots and custom chrome for his truck. A true-blue trucker is supposedly content to listen to the sound of highway being eaten up under his wheels, while a cowboy must have a stereo tape deck with country-western music to keep his gears meshing. Today's "cowboys" are the Old West's "dudes." The "truck-stop commando" in his "country Cadillac" is regarded warily by the more traditional driver in his no-nonsense rig.

There is much regional pride among truckers. Like cowboys who wore their hats creased at different angles to identify which part of the country they were from, truckers identify themselves by Rebel flags sewn on their shirts or Lone Stars embroidered on their boots. The constant criss-crossing of trucks from east to west has not broken down the ethnocentric loyalties among truckers. If anything, it has reinforced them. A southern driver is more apt to act like a redneck north of the Mason-Dixon line than down home. It is a way of identifying oneself in encounters that never last long enough for deep acquaintances to be developed. A California gearjammer waiting for a load in Connecti-

6

cut will recognize a friend in another Californian. They may spend a whole evening reminiscing about their home state, while in actuality, they are lucky to see California more than once a month.

Southern truckers are disdainful of northerners. Westerners think easterners don't know how to drive, and most everyone thinks Californians are crazy. The men who drive the incredible roads of the Alcan feel they could give lessons to everyone. Old truckers, like old wranglers, enjoy putting the fear of God into newcomers with elaborately embellished tales of jackknives on icy roads, or bridges collapsing from heavy loads.

Women truckers have their own unique problems. They have been around since the earliest days of trucking, but they are still treated as descendants of Calamity Jane. They are tolerated and even admired by some, but they remain outsiders. Women are the islands of safety and comfort to the trucker-cowboy, and he is, above all else, an unceasing romantic. Whatever might be the trucker's treatment of his own woman, the idea of women in an abstract sense demands great respect and gallantry. The ideal woman should remain pink, perfumed, and uncalloused. To most male gearjammers, women truckers are neither really women nor really truckers. They may be competent in every respect, but it is the stubborn refusal to bring women down from the pedestal, more than male chauvinism, that keeps the trucking sexes apart.

Life on the road calls for a cast-iron stomach. The cowboy's meals consisted mainly of meat and coffee. The coffee wasn't always good, but it was invariably hot and strong. The coffee that is served at most truck stops is nicknamed "hundred-mile brew," because, served triple strength, it will keep you awake for about a hundred miles to the cup. Some truck-stop coffee is brewed "western style," meaning it's been on the range all day. Along with the coffee, meat and potatoes are the staples of the trucker's diet. It's enough to make your gut bend over double, and with a few bennies for dessert, a gearjammer feels like he can drive forever. Of course, there are truckers who never take pills, just as there were cowboys who never took a drink. But the image of hard-driving and hard-living men remains. The hours are the same, too—twenty-four a day. The trucker's home is his truck, the road his porch, and the diner his kitchen. The cowboy had his prairie, and he would touch home every four months or so, when the cattle drive was over and he had delivered somebody else's goods for a price. But pretty soon the ranch house or cabin that seemed so inviting would become cramped, and he would grow

8

He's a cowboy, not a trucker
They're easy to tell apart
A cowboy's got his novelties
A trucker's got his heart.

Old cowboy listens to his stereo tape
Or his CB to check the road
Trucker sits back and listens to the wheels
Rolling in the load.

Jack Hamilton
Truckdriver

9

10

Pinballing the night away

12

claustrophobic waiting for the next drive to begin. Between drives, he would occupy himself with talk and stories; legends about the best whorehouse, the best gun, the best bar, and the shared belief that the very best was always down the next road.

When the time comes to get back on the trail, the trucker who most resembles the wrangler of the 1800s is the bull hauler. Congregating at the stockyards of Joliet, Illinois, the bull haulers, with their tight-lipped, leathery faces and crusty, worn cowboy boots, wait for their loads. The truckers are in charge of loading and unloading the cattle, as well as driving them to their destinations. Frequently, a cow with a broken back or a smashed leg must be dragged behind the pens and shot. Leaning on the fence, gazing out over an acre of cows softly shifting and mooing in their pens, the bull-hauling trucker engages in a sparse and anachronistic dialogue with his fellow cowboys.

The aura of the Old West extends to the highlight of many a trucker's year—the annual American Trucking Associations' Roadeo. It is a test of skill and reflexes decided by the handling of horsepower rather than horseflesh. The Roadeo is a gathering of truckers from all around the country. The events begin much like a rodeo, with a parade of truckers in their trucks decked out in flashy western garb. The trucks are polished to a mirror finish, and the truckers, often accompanied by their wives, wear pink, blue, gold, and black rodeo outfits. When it is time for the events, these golden boys of the world of trucking coax their rigs through a series of obstacle courses until a winner is chosen. There may be any number of drivers on the road who drive as well as the Roadeo winners, but it is doubtful if there are any as square-jawed and clean-living.

Most precious to both cowboys and truckers is the freedom to move. Any man with the ability to take that freedom away from them is a natural enemy. A state trooper or a sheriff, face shadowed by the broad brim of an official hat, is a constant menace. A trucker operating within the law may have little to fear from the police, but still they serve as an unpleasant reminder of how dear his freedom is to him. Cowboys and truckers often neglect their health because getting up properly requires staying in one place too long. The sacrifice of committing themselves to a dental chair or hospital bed usually isn't worth the results. A trucker would rather take his chances on the road than stay home with his wife and kids. Sniper attacks, shut-downs, or icy roads are always preferable to four walls.

The dangers of life on the road haven't disappeared; they have only changed. It is unlikely a trucker would be ambushed by desperadoes, but he might be hijacked by a syndicate or rolled by an innocent-looking hitch-hiker. He might be leaned on heavily by some company muscle. If trucking sounds dangerous, it is. The odds of driving a million miles or more without an accident are slim. But the idea of a nine-to-five desk job scares him silly, and the trucker usually feels that his freedom is worth the risk.

Roy Rogers and Dale Evans might well have set the stage for the husband-and-wife trucking teams of today. Gene Autry may have pointed the way to singing truckers like Red Simpson and Dick Curless. Cowboys created the legends we are familiar with today by encapsulating their thoughts and experiences into songs and stories. And they became good at shaving away the vulnerable aspects of those they admired and inflating them into bigger-than-life heros. It might seem that the cowboy's descendant, the tough, hard-driving trucker, is not at all introspective or aware of his fantasies, but the image is misleading. Truckers are poets without words. They are dreamers. Cowboys sang to their horses, they sang to their cows. But the most beautiful ballads were written to a feeling, a space, or a passage of time. The sound of a gear shifting or a long white line being eaten up and spewed out behind is the trucker's poetry. It is a ritual, and like any ritual, it cannot be analyzed by its practitioners, lest the magic vanish.

A truck gears up like a horse rears up, and with a thermos or a canteen full of hot coffee, the trucker is ready to pull out on the long trail again. The town recedes into the distance, and the trucker rides away, although not always into the sunset. There may be a girl left behind, and there might be one waiting near the phone in some town along the route. The phone is quicker than the long waits of a year or more for a letter to arrive in the Old West, but even a phone call can't always relieve the loneliness. The one thing that does relieve it is movement, and this has always been the only answer for both cowboy and truckdriver.

A photograph of the real Billy the Kid or Wild Bill Hickok is a disconcerting disappointment. They seem small and young and their clothes don't fit. You are suddenly face to face with bad teeth or a big nose. The reality can never match the legend, and it is the trucker's legend that is interesting. Don't examine a trucker too carefully. Unfocus your eyes a little and listen. Don't notice that some teeth are missing, his fingernails are dirty and his face unshaven. Instead, sit back and listen to his stories and try to imagine how he feels when he pulls his forty-ton rig up a steep grade and sails down the other side.

His History

The history of our country is a saga of motion. It is the story of a nation infatuated with pulling up stakes and moving on. We are a people who wash off past failures along with the dust of the road, people who believe the best surroundings are the ones that change, the best home is the one that moves, and the best friends are the ones we'll meet tomorrow.

This frontier individualism is the basis of much of our cultural heritage. The songs, poems, and stories that have been called "American" are the products of fresh horizons. The strength and roughness of their style expresses itself with a pure joy; the joy of motion, the joy of freedom.

The urge to move became an economic as well as romantic compulsion with the westward expansion. The difficulties that the pioneers faced and overcame —bad roads, hostile Indians, lack of food and water— became the inspiration for generations of men who learned to persevere.

The real spirit of the Old West lay not in the brocade character of men like Buffalo Bill or Wyatt Earp, but rather with the homespun farmers and everyday laborers who faced the boredom and loneliness of an untamed land. The most adventurous were the stagecoach drivers and the wagonmasters. It was their job to supervixe the transportation of hundreds of people across a hostile land. In his day the wagonmaster did not inspire the awe reserved for explorers like Lewis and Clark. He didn't even get the satisfaction of arriving at a final destination like the settlers he escorted. He was a professional guide, an explorer who would, at the end of each trip, turn around and head back.

For the wagonmaster leading people to a homestead, or the cowboy leading cattle to market, the obstacles were the same. The logbook that today's trucker must keep and the old cattleman's diary both describe a treacherous journey across hostile territory, be the writer at the mercy of Comanches or state troopers on the warpath.

Except for the cattle drives, transportation until the 1850s was uncommercial. The wagon trains were finally organized by the settlers as a form of self-protection. But there were not yet enough people living in the western parts of the continent to necessitate an effective system of transportation. Most produce was shipped by steamboat or ocean vessel, and then carried inland by irregular stagecoach trips. The stagecoach driver was the target for hijackers and Indian attacks, and the valuables he carried in his strongbox as well as the women who went west to seek their marital destinies were enticing booty for outlaws. The man who rode shotgun on the stagecoach also served as a co-driver. The term "shotgun" driver is still used by truckers, and, although less common today, hijackers are a real danger to the trucker hauling a valuable load like cigarettes or copper ingots.

As the population increased and the voice of the west grew louder, the government began to send survey crews westward to search for railroad routes, and the railroads moved from fantasy to iron reality. The men who once rode the prairies soon rode the rails.

Come all ye bold wagoneers turn out man by man
That's opposed to the railroad, or any such plan
'Tis once I made money driving my team
But the goods are now hauled on the railroad by
  steam.

—American folk song

When the golden spike was driven at Promontory, Utah, on May 10, 1869, America's wanderlust had a new vehicle and with it a new hero. He was Casey Jones, the driver of Old 97 and the inhabitant of the Big Rock Candy Mountain. America went railroad-mad.

Life on "Railroad Avenue" started to blossom into legend, giving birth to its own language and customs. Overloaded trains would "walk the dog" (jump the tracks) when driven too fast. The "shack" (conductor) would chase the "gandy dancers" (workers) who would hustle when the "boomers hit the peck" (the boss would arrive). Every small boy's dream was to be an engineer on a roaring locomotive.

The steam engine was a thing of beauty with a spirit all its own. Boys who ran away to ride the rails were out to prove themselves against a giant with a will of iron. The train was a seductress; the railroad man would be her master or victim. The train was demanding, frightening in its consumption of raw power, and awesome in its ability to convert fuel into speed. The laziness of a riverboat or the flesh-and-blood weakness of a horse could not compare with the brute strength of a locomotive highballing down the tracks. The train inspired songs, poems, and stories rivaled in imaginative extravagance only by the cowboy's heritage. The hypnotic chug of the train and the thick, black smoke bellowing from its stacks filled the dreams of restless men and boys. Prudent mothers locked their sons' bedroom doors at night.

Every time a freight train makes up in the yard
Some po woman's got an achin' heart.

—American folk song

Towns sprang up at railroad crossings around the country. Speed was king, and men lost their lives in the race for more. The shining web of steel that meshed this country together was a powerful lure even to people who couldn't legally ride the trains. Matoon, Illinois, was the largest hobo center in America because it straddled the East-West junctions of four of the largest railroads. The hobos, called "bo's" by railroaders, grew in number. In 1890 there were an estimated 60,000 tramps in America. In 1921, 20,643 "undesirables" were removed from trains during the single month of October on the Southern Pacific Line. Hobo jungles flourished, and tramps like Jeff Davis who had traveled a million miles vied for the titles of rail royalty like King of the Road.

The art of moving became a science. Hobos, whose romance with motion was in the purest form, took to calculating their chances of getting from point to point mathematically. For instance, if the distance from

Cleveland to St. Louis was 535 miles, that number would be multiplied by two (the number of tracks), then by twenty (the average number of trains per day); then, dividing the product obtained by 200 (a number representing the actual track mileage patrolled by each watchman), the odds would be clearly established. They would be examined, and the hobo would make his decision.

Tramps maintained complex identification and rating systems. Like their acquired monikers or "monikas," these names were as descriptive as they were colorful. A "blinky" was a bum who had lost an eye. A "hay bag" was a female bum, and a "jungle buzzard" was the dregs of bum society. The kings of the hobo jungles, like Frisco, the Tramp Royale, often started riding the rails as early as ten years of age. Many of the major tramps had young boys traveling with them called "proosians" who, like Fagin's students, were kept in bondage learning the ways of the world. By the time they were old enough to challenge their captors for their freedom, they were granted the title "ex-proosian."

There were complicated maneuvers involved in jumping on a moving train without getting killed. The minor goal was to get where you wanted to go. The major goal was to leave your name in as many places as possible, like the graffiti riders on the New York subways. Perhaps the most famous rail stiff of all was "A No. 1." He claimed to have traveled 200 million miles on seven dollars and twenty-eight cents, and left his moniker on every water tower and overpass from Portland, Maine, to Portland, Oregon.

Accompanying the hobos, who subsisted on a Mulligan Stew made of "hoppins" (stolen vegetables) and "gumps" (stolen chickens) were the rail-riding dogs. They were elevated to the ranks of celebrities. Betty

Lou, a little Boston Bulldog who carried her overnight bag in her mouth, held the world's record for canine travel. She is alleged to have gone over a million miles, until she was accidentally shot by a yard worker who thought she was a common pug.

At the height of the railroad craze, anybody connected with the iron monsters, no matter how nefarious their relationship, was a likely candidate for idolatry. Train robbers from Jesse James to John Harms, the last train bandit in the 1920s, all became legendary figures. The commandeering of a train, even for foul purposes, was an art worthy of recognition. The melodramatic nature of these robberies and the constant battle between engineer and desperado had its roots in the stagecoach era, and foreshadowed trucker legends about driver vs. hijacker. Train robbers, like hobos, were often men who were victims of rackets, strikes, and depressions. Like the Okies and Arkies who set out by automobile in the Depression to escape the dustbowl, the train barnacles were seeking a fast escape.

It was one of the few times in American history that blacks, whites, Chinese, and Irish immigrants worked side by side. Stories of men like "Daddy Joe," the legendary black Pullman porter, or John Henry, the bigger-than-life steel driver, are woven into the same fabric that includes railworker Paddy, and Zack the Mormon engineer. The railroad was a great leveler, and changed the lives of men from John Hay Whitney to A No. 1.

Paralleling the growth of the railroads was the automobile industry. Shortly after the turn of the century, America was feeling the first twinges of an infatuation that was to blossom into an enduring love affair with the internal combustion engine. But cars were only equipped for private use, and trains were restricted by the tracks they traveled. There was a need for a vehicle with greater mobility than a train and more strength than a car. Thus the truck was born. And the first one to roll off the ramp was not exactly a smashing success.

18

Trucks replace trains for hauling the circus to town

International speed truck 1921

The first truck on record was entered in the famous "Cosmopolitan Speed and Endurance Test" held in New York City. The course ran twenty-five miles along the Hudson. The truck raced against other cars and proved to be an abysmal failure in both speed and endurance. The driver was booed and pelted with rotten eggs, and the cry "get a horse" rang out above the crowd. For truckers, the road to glory was still strewn with tacks. It took almost thirty years before traditionalists were willing to relegate their trusted teams of workhorses to the back yard and send old Dobbin to the great glue factory in the sky. The first trucks were not very impressive by modern standards. They were small, uncomfortable, and awkward.

By 1903, the winner of an all-truck speed race ran a solid eighty miles in a little under eight hours. Still, speed alone was not enough to convince the public that trucks were of much value. One promotional gimmick involved a man and his very pregnant wife who were given a new Knox truck and all the tools and food they would need for a year. The eager couple signed a contract saying they would drive cross country with no help along the way. They were supposed to prove that truckdriving was safe enough for a family. By the time they pulled into California, the baby had been born, they had caused the collapse of fourteen bridges, and they were near exhaustion. Interest in their trip had vanished, and their inglorious arrival went unnoticed.

By 1910 trucks were no longer novelties. A few brave men and women had decided to try the truckdriving life. Large companies like Mack, Autocar, White, Reo, Kenworth, and International were founded. Truckdriving was a new life style for the cowboy, the railroader, and the adventurer. Being a truckdriver meant that you were completely responsible for your truck. Repair shops were unknown, and once a vehicle left the factory, it never came back. A trucker's pride grew from putting two million miles on his rig and having done every repair himself. Each nut and bolt had its own personality and his engine's eccentricities were tolerated like those of a loyal wife. Old-timers don't think much of modern truckdrivers who "bring their trucks in to have the ash trays emptied."

In the early 1900s trucks were little more than car chassis with converted rear ends. There were conversion kits to turn any car into a truck. One of these antiques would be completely dwarfed by a modern forty-ton semi. There is enough rubber on one modern truck tire to make a whole set for a typical old-time truck.

By 1915 truck registration had reached 160,000 and even this growth skyrocketed during World War I. Trucks were needed for the hauling of men and munitions overseas. They also carried much-needed supplies within the United States. The trucker became a stateside hero.

Though the ranks of truckers were being quickly depleted by the war, the trucking industry wasn't suffering. It was producing eight military trucks for every civilian vehicle. The inability to get foreign parts actually made for better trucks. Until this time a truck was basically an assembly of components gathered from many sources. Forced to replace imported parts with home-grown ones, the truck industry soon created better and more modern designs.

Although trucks themselves were getting more sophisticated, the trucker's comforts were still in the dark ages. Truckdrivers zipped themselves into leather outfits to combat the cold weather and rough roads. A canvas or leather greatcoat was worn and cowboy-style hat and boots completed the outfit. Sometimes leather driving gloves were needed to prevent frostbite. Most trucks offered only a hard board for a driver's seat and another to lean back on. The only padding a driver could count on was that provided by his own anatomy. There was no heat in the cabs, and heavy curtains hung on the sides to keep the wind out. Since these curtains were not much protection against freezing drafts, a trucker usually resorted to drilling a hole through the exhaust pipe to allow hot air to blow into the cab. But in the steamy months, the metal cab became a sauna on eighteen wheels, as there was no way to shut off this improvised heater.

Hard seats and icy weather weren't the only headaches. Headlights in those days were small presto carbide lamps that gave off a candlelight glow. The lamps were enclosed in fragile glass globes that were easily broken by rocks or pebbles in the road. In stormy weather, the problems multiplied. Window wipers had not yet been invented, and truckers often used a raw potato and saltpeter to glaze the window against the rain.

As companies like Mack and Kenworth became well established in the 1920s, seat cushions replaced boards, and doors replaced curtains as standard equipment. Mack Trucks was founded by Jack Mack, who ran away from home at age ten to work as a teamster. Jack and his brother Augustus had been experimenting as early as 1878 with the idea of building a truck. The prototypes were not always successful, and most of the Mack brothers' early inventions found their way to the bottom of the East River.

Biscuit Jones

Casey Jones was a brave engineer
And perhaps the greatest in the land
But he was not the only Jones
To become a railroad man.

Biscuit Jones was a cook by trade
Before he took to riding the rail
But he couldn't stand being told what to do
So he hit the silver trail.

In his day there was a rock oven
In his camp along the rail
You could always tell his camp
By that home-baked smell.

Thus he became known as "Biscuit"
By every "Bo" along the line
I was proud to say ole Biscuit
Was surely a friend of mine.

I was with him in the baggage car
That day of the fatal run
He had that oven fired to perfection
And those biscuits were almost done.

Ole Casey hollered "There's a Southbound comin'
Jump or we'll all be dead"
But Biscuit said "Y'all go on
I just can't leave this bread."

Now somewhere there's a rock oven
Lying in that railroad sand
With a sign that reads
"Here lies Homer Lee Jones
That Railroadin' biscuit man."

Jack Hamilton

22

Mack's emblem, the bulldog, has always been associated with trucking, but it wasn't until the 1930s that it became official. Colonel Alfred Masary, a chief engineer at Mack, designed the famous radiator ornament that became Mack's mascot. He got the idea from the affectionate nickname "the bulldog truck" that the British gave to the strange American vehicle with its blunt nose and low growl.

In the early 1930s, the truckdriver back in America was still seeing hard times. There was no such thing as a truck stop, and hardly any facilities for showering or sleeping. In warm weather the trucker rigged a hammock under his trailer or he slept on top of the truck, or, if it was raining, on the ground under the trailer. There wasn't any room to lie down inside the cab. If he was lucky, he would find a bunk house for the night and a hot meal for a dollar. News of the best places to stop was passed on by word of mouth, as were the early songs and tall tales of truckers' exploits. The Interstate system had not yet been built, and the roads were two-lane, and mostly dirt covered. The trucks were still gas fueled, and a trucker had to carefully navigate his route from gas pump to gas pump. Money was tight, and many men gave up their homes to travel full time in their trucks. The truckers' renaissance came at the unlikely time of the Depression, when the diesel engine was invented and the sound and scope of the trucking world was drastically changed.

With the more complicated instrumentation of the diesel engine, truck dashboards began to resemble small jet planes. Cabs were equipped with roll-up glass windows, seats with springs and hot water heaters for comfort. The humidity and heat inside was more conducive to growing orchids than to truckdriving, but it was an improvement. As trucks grew more complicated, so did the truckdriver's life. Trucking was now big business, founded on the money of men like J. P. Morgan, who bailed out Mack Trucks during the Depression.

When the money started to flow, so did the bureaucratic red tape. Safety commissions were established, and by 1935 the Motor Carrier act was passed to control interstate transport. Truckers now needed official sanctions to operate and cross state lines. The establishment of the Interstate Commerce Commission shook the industry to the bones. Drivers were hired and fired, lives and property were threatened by militant groups on both sides, and almost everybody was dead broke. Nobody seemed to know who or what could drive, and strikes and shutdowns were the result.

The government had tried to limit the trucker's freedom to move, and wasn't ready for the backlash. About the only time a trucker voices his opinions is if he is made to stay in one place too long.

Despite the grumblings of the drivers, the industry was really trucking along. The trucker was being portrayed by Humphrey Bogart in the film *They Drive by Night*. The public had recognized the trucker as a professional with a unique style and was fascinated with his exploits.

Trucks were being designed to enable the driver to make his truck a home on wheels. The sleeper cab was offered for the first time as the result of the loud complaints voiced by a single gearjammer from Seattle. The driver had complained to the Kenworth Company that the bed in the trailer where he slept when his co-driver was at the wheel would shake so badly that he felt he was going to break his back. The Kenworth Company developed a cab for a truck that had a bed placed behind the driver's seat. The trucker was so happy with the results that he became a one-man advertising campaign, and Kenworth was deluged with requests for trucks with sleepers. It became possible for team drivers to double their time by alternating drivers while one slept in relative comfort. Truck designers began to experiment with new designs originally developed during World War II. The turbine engine was tried, but discarded when diesels proved more practical. All-aluminum engines were adopted because of their lightness.

By the 1950s trucks began to reflect the fashion spirit of the times. Women wore sack dresses, cars wore pointed fins, and poodles were dyed pink. The color of the year was "breen," a cross between brown and green, and the truck of the year was the "bruck," a cross between a truck and a bus. Truckers' complaints of poor visibility caused an over-eager designer to produce the Cab-Beside-Engine design. In the C.B.E. the driver is housed in a tiny compartment to the extreme right of the engine. The truck appeared to have lost one half of itself. The only way for a passenger to ride was suspended on a canvas sling in the back of the driver. This white elephant was a new low in both comfort and practicality.

The truckdriver's image also changed in the fifties. Instead of Humphrey Bogart, he was now portrayed by Mario Lanza, a singing trucker in *That Midnight*

Kiss. Leather driving suits were replaced by blue jeans and Eisenhower jackets. The trucker's accessories included a long purse with a zipper, called a chain-drive pocketbook, and the obligatory belt buckle inscribed with the driver's name and perhaps his truck. During this time, the use of amphetamines increased, as portrayed with suitably grisly results in the Chuck Conners B-movie *Death in Small Doses*. Slang names like "West-Coast turnarounds," "black mollies," or "bennies" became the popular inside code.

Truck stops were built at a rapid pace to keep up with the growing demand. Truckers no longer had to worry about fitting their trucks on the cement apron at some roadside cafe. Now they had to keep two steps ahead of the tourists who had learned that "truckdrivers know all the good places to eat." The drivers constituted such a large body of workers that organizations like the American Trucking Associations were formed to help voice their opinions as a group, and the teamsters union provided the muscle behind that voice.

Drivers who drove for the love of the road either had to learn the new rules or quit the game. Gypsy drivers, those men who trucked without permits or authority, faced stiff penalties if caught. The trucker had become a common carrier, and by 1975 the gross revenue of trucking carried by the nation's 21 million men and women truckdrivers was almost $23 billion a year.

Truckdriving has come of age. A fully equipped, forty-ton eighteen-wheeler costing close to $60,000 is a far cry from its early ancestors. The driver, usually mortgaged to his ears with small business loans, sometimes drives day and night just to keep ahead. Endless drifts of paperwork often dampen his spirit. Logbooks, fuel tickets, and mileage records can dull the raw exhilaration of just plain driving. But in spite of the fact that the government sees him as a common carrier who must navigate his way around mountains of paperwork, a trucker can still see himself as the last American cowboy.

Wander into any of the little stores in Scrubgrass County, Pennsylvania, and someone will be able to tell you where Willie Cocoanut lives. Willie is known as Apache Bill to the truckdrivers who pass his house daily. Apache Bill was born around the time the first truck rolled off the assembly line and as he approaches his seventieth birthday, he can see from his front porch overlooking Interstate 80 the changes trucks and truckdrivers have gone through.

Bogie coffees up in "They Drive by Night"

25

Apache Bill

Apache Bill got his name from being, he claims, Geronimo's great-grandson. His grandfather drove a wagon train west in the 1800s. En route, the story goes, he kidnapped Geronimo's daughter. She learned to live in the world of white settlers, producing a number of children for him, including Apache Bill's mother. Bill's grandfather kept a diary documenting his travels, written on buffalo hide. Apache Bill now keeps the old diary in a tin box along with his grandmother's beaded headband, old coins, and other memorabilia.

Apache Bill was born in 1908, with two generations of traveling blood in his veins. His home was a small ranch forty miles northeast of Pahuska, Oklahoma, in what was then called the Cherokee nation. The only proof of his birth is recorded in his mother's Bible. His father died when he was a child, and his mother, preoccupied with raising his other brothers and sisters, was not much concerned when the urge to wander hit him as a teenager. Inspired by his grandfather's tales, he sought adventure as a truckdriver in the early 1920s.

"When I first started out, trucking was different than it is today. Everything was moved by horse or jackass and wagon from the railroad stations. Things may have come a long way, but come to think of it, I still know a lot of jackasses who are hauling goods. It used to take days to go places that now only take a few hours. Diesel was six gallons for a dollar. The speed limit was thirty and fifteen in town. Now they back up that fast."

Bill can't remember how many trucks he has owned in his lifetime, but he fondly remembers his first—a 1927 Model T. He has retired trucks with a million miles on them, and there are some whose rusted orange-brown carcasses still recline comfortably like old friends around his property. The tiny farmhouse he lives in is distinguished from its rural neighbors by the hand-painted letters on the side of the barn announcing "Apache Bill's Funny Farm—the rest home of a tired trucker." Old trucks, cattle skulls, signs warning bill collectors to stay out, Rebel flags, and assorted oddities embroider the terrain. In the winter Apache Bill seals off the rest of the house and lives with his fifteen-year-old Chihuahua in the kitchen, easily heated by a pot-bellied stove.

Apache Bill

Checking channel 10 for eighteen-wheelers

Bill has led a bachelor's existence for the last thirty-two years, and like many solitary old men who establish their own everyday routines, his is slightly eccentric. Every kitchen implement has its own nail to hang on, and shares the wall space with girlie calendars from the 1950s and novelty items like "Polish" pistols with barrels that point in the wrong direction. On the kitchen table rests his prize possession—a CB radio. Phone-less and often snowed-in in the winter, Apache Bill depends on it as his main link with the world—or at least those in the world who still interest him—the truckdrivers who roll by his door. Weaving their way across country they blink their headlights at his farm; some out of respect and love for the old man who pioneered the kind of life they live, some out of curiosity, attracted by the strange slogans visible from the Interstate, and some in desperation, looking for help in an accident.

Once in a while a woman trucker will find her way to Apache Bill's door. He remembers these occasions with glee. All his life Bill has been a ladies' man, a condition he attributes to being half Indian and half Scorpio. He was married once, in 1942, to a senorita he met while trucking in Chihuahua, Mexico. He had blown the rear end of his truck and, while waiting for another to come from the states, he fell in love. His independent nature dismissed the legal technicalities of the wedding ceremony, and he asked a fellow trucker whom he dubbed "Father José" to perform the ceremony. With the truck's rear end newly mended and festooned with Mexican good luck streamers, Bill and his bride entered the U.S. The new wife lasted only a few trips across the country in his truck before she disappeared with another trucker one night in Minnesota. Bill, delighted with the new arrangement, gave up married life forever.

Like most truckers, Apache Bill has enough sex and adventure stories to last through many nights of serious drinking. The ragged scar on his white-haired belly is a souvenir of a lonely birthday celebrated in bed with two bloodthirsty hookers. The broken mattress in the bedroom is the result of the 300-pound woman trucker who, with her girl friend, ran wild through his home one weekend. His memories are little islands of delight strung together like backroads on a familiar map.

A retired million-miler Ol' 97

31

THE FUNNY FARM

REST HOME
FOR A TIRED
TRUCKER

A "Tired Truckers" retreat

32

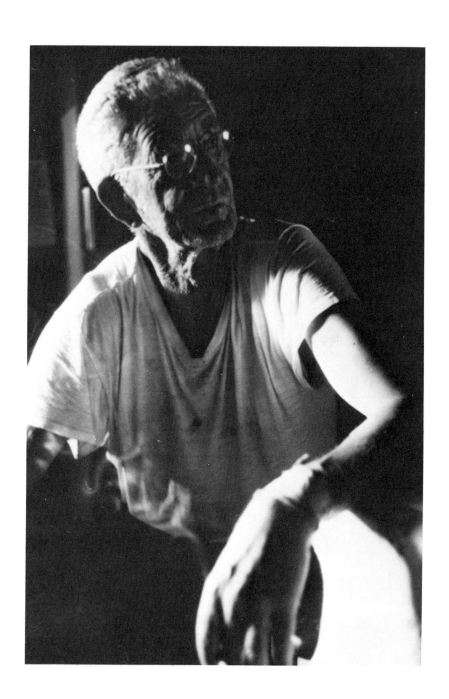

Bill is concerned about his old dog's health, and he is apt to doze off with her on his lap while he talks on the CB radio. He is getting too old to travel with the hundreds of truckers who still offer him rides. His bones ache for the comforts of home after sitting for hours in a truck. But some friends like Cowboy Jack can still occasionally seduce him out onto the road with their glorious new rigs.

He admits with mixed feelings that he is looked after by the smokies who cruise the highway outside his home. The troopers will notice when he hasn't been broadcasting on his radio, and stop by his house to check on him. Other times they trade things—a box of road flares for a basket of fresh garden vegetables. Sometimes they tell him of a stranded trucker down the highway who needs a place to stay for the night. It is these times Apache Bill likes the best—times shared with other truckers—when he can trade stories and memories, as the diesels roll past his door, their rumble fading into the night.

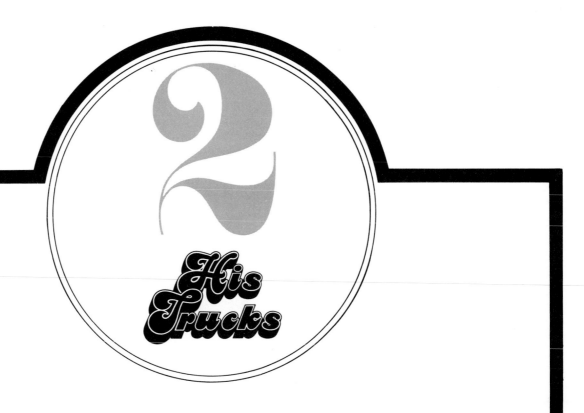

His Trucks

There'd be no truckdrivers if it wasn't for us trucks
No double-clutching gearjamming coffee-drinking nuts
They drive their way to glory
And they have all the luck
There'd be no truckdrivers if it wasn't for us trucks.

The wind comes up fast in the midwest. Tonight it's flying low down the center of the two-lane blacktop. Cold gusts filter through a rusted truck chassis lying by the side of the road, nothing left but a decayed frame with the skeletons of two air seats, their brittle brown leather skins pulled taut. It's the beginning of another long trucker's night, the kind of night a man needs his truck to comfort him. He wants to be soothed by the hum of the engine and flattered by his mastery of its strength.

Down Highway 65 a truck is making its way east. The wind snakes in and around its radiator grill whistling as it shoots off fans of gravel from the road and small bugs meet their death on its flat windscreen. The flames from its twin chromed stacks light up the night sky, and its throaty rumble reverberates in the Indiana air.

The man at the wheel of this truck may not be married, but he's probably mortgaged up to his ears supporting forty tons of rubber and steel. He's taken out a small business loan to buy the rig and, like thousands of others on the road, he's been shelling out better than five hundred a month for the privilege. Truckdrivers make good money, but it takes long hours and a lot of heartache and loneliness to make it pay. You sacrifice love and comfort for the $18,000-plus a year, and the money will probably go into your next truck anyway. Pretty soon the lines creep into your face so fast it's like watching a time-lapse film.

The lights of the truck stop up ahead shine like a desert oasis, and you wonder when it will all be over. How many miles before the long haul is through? But you know the payments on the truck and the emptiness in your pocket are just excuses for a journey that may never end. The feel of that gearshift in your hand has made too deep an impression for you to stop now.

What makes a bunch of metal screws and nuts and plating suddenly take on such presence? The same thing that makes flesh and bone and cartilage into a person. The truck has a soul. It can be a devil or an angel or just a trusted companion on a long haul. A truck gone wild can be a twisted nightmare, hurling you headlong into the center rail with a front-wheel blow-out, or it can be as gentle as a mother's love, rocking you to sleep on its softly padded belly.

There are almost as many types of truckers as there are trucks, but most of them are either the "nine-to-fivers" or long-haulers. Some travel the local roads, delivering furniture or produce, and covering little more than 300 miles a day. They sleep in their own beds at night—or at least every other night—and they can remember their kids' ages without too much figuring. This type of trucker usually drives a company truck and is not subject to the same pressures that the long-haulers face.

The long-hauling over-the-road driver may be a wild-catting owner-operator or a teamster driving a company truck. Either way his truck is his first home. If he is one of the 100,000 owner-operators in the country, the hard core of independent trucking, then he truly is the last American cowboy—a man whose freedom to move has no bounds. His possessions may be in cold storage waiting until he has trucked his last load. If he is married and has a few kids, he will be lucky to see them every few weeks. The long-hauler can make very good money, his income often matching many New York executives. But more often than not, he is living on credit, since his money goes right back into his truck, or to help his friends, or maybe just to buy cheap junk at the truck stop to send home to his wife and kids. The long-hauler will put a million miles on

37

Eighteen Wheels a Walkin'

I got eighteen wheels a walkin'
I got a 318 a talkin'
Headin' down to Georgia
Goin' home on my mind.

As this big diesel keeps a hummin'
My mind keeps a runnin'
Right back down to Georgia'
And that gal a waitin' down the line.

Well I pulled out of Georgia
Eight long weeks ago
The night I left it was freezing
And just startin' to snow.

But I knew I had to pull that trailer
If I was to pay my bills on time
So I kissed Mama and headed that diesel
Straight for the old state line.

I got stopped in Louisiana
Running overload
By the time I made California
I was three weeks on the road.

I'd been stopped in five or six states
I had been across
Not to mention all the times
Me and that diesel got lost.

Well I finally made it into Frisco
Right down by that old Golden Gate
But that dock boss told me "Son we don't take it
When you get it here two weeks late."

He was just about to tell me to turn it around
And take it on back down South
But I dumped that load and turned it around
Before he could open his mouth.

Now I got eighteen wheels a walkin'
I got a 318 a talkin'
Headin' back down to Georgia
Going home on my mind.

As this big diesel keeps a hummin'
My mind keeps a runnin'
Right back down to Georgia
And that gal waitin' down the line.

Jack Hamilton
Truckdriver

his truck before it is retired. He travels coast to coast in the time most people take to travel one-quarter of the distance. His truck is his profession, and claims most of his money and the best of his dreams.

The basic over-the-road truck is a tractor and trailer joined at the "fifth wheel" by a long nail-shaped rod called the "kingpin." The trailer is the utilitarian part of the vehicle where the load is carried. The tractor, also referred to as the cab, is the soul of the truck. Here the driver lavishes his money and his imagination. The cost of an everyday truck is staggering when compared to a Volkswagen or even a Cadillac. Many trucks on the road today cost more than a nice home. The tractor alone can run anywhere from $20,000 to $60,000, depending on the make and the driver's passion for chrome. The trailer can cost another $15,000, and from there the possibilities for customizing are endless.

When a truckdriver buys a new rig he's buying style, performance, and ride. The traditional long-nosed "conventional" is eye-catching, with its enormous hood extended like an iron fist. Drivers say it's a smoother-riding truck, with more protection in an accident. Others, like Jack from Iowa, swear by a flat-faced, pug-nosed "cabover." "I like to be right up front in a truck. Hell, I don't want to be lookin' over some fancy hood ornament on a long-nose, when I could be seeing something dangerous on the road that might kill me." In a cabover the driver actually sits over the engine, which, despite the insulation and heavy padding, throws up a strong vibration. Between the driver and the "shotgun seat" is a large padded hump called the "dogbox." In spite of its layers of foam rubber and insulation, the dogbox does little to muffle the noise that echoes in a trucker's ears long after he has pulled into his favorite diner.

When Jack is at the wheel of his new Peterbilt, he can look down at the thirteen gauges on the dashboard. There are sixteen forward gears to shift, eighteen tires, and a big Cat-powered diesel engine to make the truck roll. The top-of-the-line trucks—the Kenworths, the Peterbilts, the Marmons, and the Reos—are truly magnificent. Awesome in size and performance, they each cost as much as four top-of-the-line Cadillacs or a couple of super Maseratis.

Unlike a car, a truck may house one of a number of engine-transmission combinations. A Mack truck may have a Maxidyne engine, a Detroit Diesel, or a Cat-powered model. The engine can range in power from a modest 180 horsepower into the 400s and a few select 600-plus models, called "Purple People Eaters"

40

Peterbilt assembly line
Madison, Tennessee
(right)

for their custom lavender paint jobs. If purple's not your passion, and you still want a mighty rig, Detroit Diesel can supply you with 1472 cubic inches displaced by 16 cylinders generating 680 horsepower. Since shifting gears is really what trucking is all about, a driver gets pretty damn good at it. Most truckers make use of the clutch pedal only as they first ease out onto the road. Once above low gear, the sound of the engine is all they need to guide them through the full range of gears without once hitting the clutch. Just try this kind of driving on a simple four-speed transmission and you will soon appreciate the trucker's skill with his sixteen gears.

To the car driver, all semis look alike. But just as there is a world of difference between a Volkswagen and a Rolls-Royce, the type of truck a man drives speaks volumes to other truckers. An inexpensive cab often means a company driver, or a man who hasn't been able to make those long hauls and longer hours pay off for him. He must be content to command a rig that will never turn any heads when he pulls into a truck stop. While the modest truck may house a real dedicated road-lover, it's clear that he can't afford the time or money that the owner of a $70,000 machine is willing to pour into his rig.

The genesis of a truck's image can be traced as far back as the workshop of a truck designer like Bob Carrier. Bob lives with his Keeshond Kim and his horse Sweetface on a small ranch in East Texas. Bob loves truckers and the trucks he designs for them. "A good truck designer must know how to drive a truck," says Bob, "Not only on a test track, but on the open road and for weeks at a time."

To design the housing for a professional traveler is a grand responsibility. The designer helps shape the truckdriver's ego by doling out the flash and luxury. But truck designers—even good ones like Bob Carrier—create only the basics, and no matter how sumptuous the basics may seem, there is no limit to the customizing that can bring the basic truck to the heights of freewheeling glory.

When all is said and done, no matter how a truck looks, it's the power of sixteen forward gears that ignites the diesel fuel in a trucker's veins. Unlike a car, a truck may have more than one gearbox. Older trucks required the driver to use both hands in order to shift gears. The main gearbox controls the speed, and the auxiliary box (called the "auxbox" by drivers) controls the level of that speed, breaking it into high and low. There can be a total speed range of eight to twenty gears, manipulated by the trucker, who might wear his

traditionally white split-shifting gloves and his gear-jamming boots. A trucker with both hands on the sticks, and his arm threaded through the steering wheel, maneuvering a forty-foot van along a strip of concrete, cannot help but feel like a king stud in a world of gear-stripping, lane-hogging commoners.

When he can't keep his eyes open a minute longer, and he pulls off the road for some shuteye, the type of truck he has chosen determines a driver's accommodations for the night. A conventional truck is equipped with what is often referred to as a "suicide box." The suicide box is a sleeper that is attached in back of the cab, and is entered by crawling through a small space where the cab's rear window would normally be. Some sleepers are "pajama boxes," entered through a side door which for a large man or woman can be a lot easier than trying to thread through a nineteen-by-twenty-nine-inch space.

Once inside the sleeper, the derivation of the name "suicide box" becomes clear. Except for a narrow air vent and the crawlway window, the sleeper is a completely sealed off area. In a luxurious truck, it will be padded with roll-and-tuck Naugahyde. In a cheaper model it will be less padded, making for more road noise and vibration. The bunk runs the entire width of the truck. The bed's length is 80 inches, the same as a bed at home, and the width can be ordered up to 110 inches across.

Mighty Me and Charlie are drivers from Santa Fe. They have a cabover with a queen-size sleeper that has been the source of endless arguments from the first day out. Mighty Me and Charlie are "married"—they are co-drivers who don't change partners. "Christ," says Mighty Me, "The goddamned bed sheets are on wrong." Charlie, who has a habit of putting sheets on upside down, returns with his usual challenge, "If ya don't like it, find yourself another driver. He'll probably run the damn rig off the road, but your sheets will look pretty." Like most married drivers, they fight like fishwives after ten minutes on the road, and most fights concern the truck. "I sleep better in my truck than I do at home," says Charlie. "Sometimes my wife will wake up and find me on the living room couch. She thinks I'm crazy, but it feels more like my truck to me."

The sleeper has not always been a part of the cab. Around the 1940s they were installed in some rather unlikely places around the truck. At one time, the sleeper was placed under the truck where the spare tire is now carried. In addition to looking like a minstrel in blackface from the dirt of the road blowing on him, the passenger in the sleeper was unable to communicate with the driver. He had no way to let his partner

42

43

44

know if he wanted to stop. To solve this problem, an emergency brake was placed in the bunk. If the man inside wanted to stop the truck, he would pull up the brake and pray that nobody was tailgating.

Trucker John Laney of Monroe, North Carolina, remembers the fate of one fat gearjammer who was dozing in a different type of sleeper, a mattress placed in a niche carved in the side of the trailer. While he slept, the rig jackknifed and flipped the trailer over on its side and the man was trapped head down in the narrow bunk. As John Laney remembers it, "they had to get a crane to hoist him outta that thing. Man, he looked like a mummy—bed sheets wrapped all around him, just his feet kinda stickin' out the end. That's one fat trucker who's been sleeping in the bunkhouse ever since."

Married drivers may bitch at each other, but they aren't likely to get divorced. They have found something that is rare even in real marriages—trust. For a professional driver to sleep while another is driving is the ultimate compliment in the world of trucks.

Accidents involving the sleeper are dangerous, but more common and more feared is a front-wheel blowout. If the right wheel goes—and you're lucky—it will pull you into a ditch. If the right side of the road is the side of a mountain or a wall or another truck, you're in trouble. If the left wheel blows, you will be pulled into the fast lane of traffic or the center divider. It's bad either way, and nobody—not even the 300-pound, muscle-shirted steel-hauler—can change that truck's course. A loaded forty-foot truck creates more momentum than is comfortable to think about. When that tire explodes and you drop ten inches in a second onto the wheel rim with eighty thousand pounds pushing you at seventy miles an hour in the wrong direction, it's time to pray.

If a back tire goes, it isn't so bad. They are in groups of four, and if the inside one blows, it's a pain in the ass to fix, but you won't be fishtailing all over the road. In fact, a weakness on the "inside dual" can go undetected until it explodes, spewing black rubber over the highway. For this reason, truckers circle their truck before each long haul, beating on the tires with a tire billy to check the pressure.

The hubcap of most truck tires is eye level with the average automobile. Tire prices start at about $150 and go as high as $400 per tire for an 11.00 x 22, about the biggest tire on the road. Trucks that haul rocks or heavy materials need special tires. There are some that will tower over your head even if you are over six feet. These are capable of carrying loads of 53,000 pounds each. They are 46-ply and cost $12,000. It will

take a crew of men two days to change one. Perhaps the largest tire of all is made for earth-moving trucks. The size is 36.00 x 51. It sells for $25,596, plus tax.

How did the trucker making his way down twin ribbons of concrete choose his particular truck? What were the decisions that went into buying this vehicle that has become his home, his womb, and even his straightjacket? He chose it with as much care as you would choose a mate; a choice to live with for years to come, to sleep with at night, to maintain in sickness and in health. Each part of the truck has been carefully considered—the tires, the engine, the headlights, all hand picked. Sensitive and vulnerable, their shortcomings are the truckdriver's anguish.

A man doesn't lay down thirty or forty grand just to get from here to there. He buys that truck to make money, and he makes money by hauling things. The style of the truck, the engine and the size of the wheels, are all selected to suit the payload he will be transporting. While the cab can be as free and fancy as a first love, to make any money the driver's got to get hitched—he needs a trailer. His choice is basically between a trailer that encloses its cargo, and one on which the cargo is in the open and tied down. Livestock haulers for cows, goats, chickens, or anything still alive are always enclosed trailers.

The flat, open trailers are called "flatbeds" and a flatbed driver must be familiar with the temperamental intricacies of securing a load by tarping and strapping it down. He must reckon with strong, gusting winds that can strew his load all over the highway. Enclosed trailers are much easier to load unless they are to carry a shipment of live cargo which requires a special type of enclosure.

Herman is loading his cattle hauler at Joliet, Illinois. The inside of a livestock trailer smells worse than a New York subway at rush hour in August. Cows are herded on with the use of electric prods, kicking and bellowing in fear and anger as they pummel the metal walls. Loading a cattle trailer is a perilous job. As in bullfighting, much of the mastery of the animals depends on eye contact and hand signals punctuated by sharp noises. The tendons in Herman's arms are tensed like steel bands as he wields the prod. His co-driver was gored in the chest a month ago, and he has seen men trampled in the pens and loading chutes. Unintelligible commands are barked at the cattle, who shuffle along like huge commuters. The electric prod is used to turn them in the right direction. A thunderstorm of hooves beats the floor of Herman's metal truck and the herd presses away from one panicking animal.

Down at the other end of the Joliet complex, past the Stockman's Cafe where truckers and livestock buyers chew their hamburgers, are the pens of screaming pigs. They are being washed before loading. Some have been marked with red X's on their back to indicate final destination, and all of them are squealing with rage as torrents of water rinse the mud blankets from their backs. They are lined up and loaded too, and the electric prods are used again. Another shipment of bacon takes its first step on the road to somebody's freezer. Cattle haulers line up outside the pens for one last scrape of their boots on the shit scrapers before they climb the metal stairs to their rigs.

Once their cargo has been slaughtered and dressed, it is called swinging beef. A trucker hauling a "reefer" full of swinging beef is a high-risk driver. "If you jack-knife a load of swinging beef, or take a curve too fast, the momentum from the sides of meat will throw you right over. I've seen men killed by a side of beef that came through the back of the sleeper," says Bob, a livestock hauler from Nebraska.

Peter calls himself a bedbug hauler. He drives a furniture truck from Chicago to points east and west. He is always careful to load his double-decker truck on the "high side" to prevent the shifting of furniture during turns and stops. After an often tortuous trip across country, he must round up a crew to unload the truck. If he is in a high rate area, he will be forced to pay a small fortune for a crew consisting perhaps of a 250-pounder who feels threatened at the prospect of lifting anything heavier than a lamp, and an old man who moves with the ease of a constipated snail. Still, getting his crew into high gear is a snap compared to dealing with the people who are waiting for the furniture. According to his company's rules, he will call them to let them know when he will arrive, and to remind them to have cash or a bank check ready when he pulls up in his van. When he is presented with a personal check made out to the wrong company, he isn't surprised. Worse things have happened. He remembers the time he drove 3000 miles with a truck full of furniture only to be met by a wailing woman at the end of the line, telling him that her husband had divorced her, and could he please take the furniture back to New York, where it now legally belonged.

Peter has often bitten his tongue as the transplanted furniture owners threaten him with lawsuits or try to get him fired because the leg of their favorite chair has been broken off in transit. How are they to know that leg probably snapped off when he braked a little too hard on that icy road near Seattle, where he narrowly

Life under a Steering Wheel

Now, if you're thinking of becoming a truckdriver
There's some things I'd like to say to you.
There's a whole lot better ways of making a living
And, of course, a whole lot safer, too.
I guess you think we're just sittin' up there taking it easy
Pushing that big rig, and just takin' a ride,
But the truth is
We're just trying to keep her between the ditches
And help everybody else out there to stay alive.
Oh sure, we make pretty good money,
But I want to tell you, Mister,
We earn every cent,
And sometimes you're gone from home so long
Your dog won't know you
When you walk back through your fence.
And in the spring of the year,
You've got those tornadoes
And there's rain, and hail and dust and sand.
And in the summertime, it'll get so doggone hot
That steering wheel will even burn your hand.
Then, in the winter, it'll be that ice and snow
When nobody should be out on that road
But about one A.M. that dispatcher will call,
"O.K., Buddy, crawl out of that sack and let's roll."
Sometimes you run your fool head off.
You need a good check just to pay some bills,
And then you look at that withholding slip.
Somehow it just kinda gives you cold chills.
After twenty years, I've gone through all this
And the miles I've made you just wouldn't believe.
And the things I've seen happen out on that ol' highway
Would make a great big book
Much too thick to read.
Now, you go right ahead, Buddy, and hire out
'Cause I guess I couldn't stop you anyhow,
But if mine was to do over
I'd still be in Mississippi
Following that ol' mule
And holding on to a Georgia stock plow.

Joe West

49

avoided a jackknife which would have easily killed him and that Toyota full of college kids next to him? What does a lout of a truckdriver know about their priceless chair, that was hand-carved by Ben Franklin's second cousin?

If carrying swinging beef or livestock is risky, some loads are like entering a combat zone. Men who spend their days hauling dangerous chemicals, high explosives, or nitroglycerine are in a special, lonely class. Chemicals are usually carried in a tanker, and if especially dangerous, will have a police escort. Driving a rig with dynamite or nitro in its trailer can earn you a lot of money and a wide piece of the highway with no tailgaters, but you cut down your chances of making it to retirement. An accident involving chemicals is about the least favorite for the police or fire department. The explosion caused by a truckload of noxious gas can blow up a good-sized town, not to mention the driver.

There is a policeman living in Palo Alto who retired from the force seven years ago to sell insurance. His friend, a truckdriver, was in a crash and his truckload of acid leaked down his head and body, searing off his skin and soldering him to the asphalt road. While he begged to die, the policeman shot him through the head, ending his friend's misery and his own career.

There are trucks on the road that sparkle like the eyes of a bride on her wedding day, and there are the buckets of bolts held together by spit and a prayer. It costs twenty-five dollars to wash a truck—a fair pocketful of change for most people. But there is a woman down in Texas who operates a whole fleet of trucks that never hit the road unless they're as clean as a nun's habit. Other companies, like Monfort, which prides itself on its dazzling orange and yellow Kenworths, give each truck a good "douche job" before it goes on the road.

There are companies who send their drivers out in garbage wagons—trucks with tires as bald as Kojak's head and bunks reeking of other drivers' sweaty socks. But on the right side of the drivers are companies like Monfort, or like Freddie Hart's "Hartliners" which purchase show trucks and add them to their fleets. You can spot the "Hartliner" by it's Texas-size red heart emblazoned across the chrome cab. Down around Columbia, South Carolina, there is a company that doesn't pay as well as most, but has a waiting list of applicants as long as your arm. It purchases show trucks after every truck exposition. The "Queen of Hearts" is its latest acquisition. A customized Peterbilt, it has the playing card painted with considerable skill on either side of the radiator grill. The color scheme is red, white, and black, and the interior complements the outside design.

There are still truckers who would rather listen to the sound of the road than worry about the color scheme of their truck. But, the worshippers of Jerry Malone and the "Boss Truck" are a devoted flock. Jerry Malone is a former truckdriver. His Boss Truck rose like a phoenix from a standard 1970 Kenworth conventional. His dream was to make it the fastest and most expensive truck in the world. First he decorated it with $12,000 worth of chrome trim, then an acrylic, candy-apple hand-rubbed paint job twelve layers deep, costing $5,000. The gleam of its satin skin is blinding. The truck's fifth wheel (the coupling device used to join the tractor to the trailer) is gold-plated and perhaps some day the more than $10,000 he paid for it in 1970 will seem a bargain. But Jerry wasn't satisfied. He wanted the world's fastest truck, as well as the world's prettiest, so he installed a 12-V-71 Detroit Diesel engine with an RTO-9513 transmission. Eighteen racing tires replaced the show whitewalls. Running the Bonneville Salt Flats at 125 mph, it averages out to 114.9 mph. The truck's windshield was removed—at that speed, its glass would have blown out. The Boss Truck has no muffler, and the noise exploding from its four chromed straight stacks is a siren song for nobody but a truck-driver. All told, Jerry Malone's dream set him back $100,000. Jerry Malone and his bouffanted, blond girl friend Peggy are working on the plans for the Super Boss Truck 1975. In the meantime, Jerry Malone always has the forty-foot frozen whale that he keeps in a reefer van to show interested visitors.

The Boss Truck, when it is not racing, has another "more practical" side. It is equipped with twin sleeper boxes which have been converted into his and her play-rooms. "His" contains a bar with crystal chandeliers, champagne in a bucket, and four barstools—just right for the trucker-playboy. "Hers" plays the powder-puff role—a dressing table and chair with pink froufrou accessories and endless amounts of carpeting.

Like most truckers, Jerry Malone loves things big. The biggest rig, the most powerful engine, and the heaviest load all thrill him. The largest load ever hauled by a truck was the Saturn rocket used on the Apollo missile. The truck was kept shrouded with white cloths, and hauled in a convoy—eighty feet long and fourteen feet wide. "Moby Dick," as the rig was nicknamed, weighed in at a healthy twenty-five tons. The caravan surrounding the truck was made up of eleven armed guards, cars with loudspeakers announcing its arrival, and other vehicles with danger signs and flashing lights following in its wake. Traffic jams stretched for miles behind Moby Dick, the monster load, as it took up two full lanes of highway. The load was raised and lowered with hydraulic rams. The eastern part of the country proved most treacherous, with its curving roads and low underpasses. The air in Moby Dick's tires was let out at times to give a few extra inches of clearance for the great white whale of a truck. Altogether the truck traveled 2500 miles.

The Saturn rockets were the largest, but not the heaviest, thing ever to be moved by trucks. The heavyweight prize would have to go to an atomic generator unit weighing 145,000 pounds. The unit had to be moved a mere fifteen miles from the railroad to the plant, and a special rig was designed for that purpose. On paper the truck was an engineering masterpiece, but the journey was a nightmare. The seventy-three-ton load wound up in the bottom of a muddy canal when the road caved in. It took four months to haul it and the truck out of the river, whereupon it was promptly returned to sender.

Driving gives a man time to create a whimsical language shared only by other gearjammers, and often incomprehensible to outsiders. When a truck isn't being referred to as "she" or "my little pussycat," it is often called by its make. A Kenworth becomes a K.W. or a K-Whopper or a KantWork. A GMC is a General Mess of Crap or a Jimmy. A Freightliner is a Fruitliner. The brakes in the truck may be called Jake Brakes or the "Push and Wonder" variety—You push them and wonder if they'll work. The eighteen tires are "baloneys." If radials, they're "singing waffles." Every destination has its own special name. Los Angeles becomes the Shaky City. Boston is Beantown. San Diego is Dago. Everyone a trucker meets will be labeled, too, from the "connivin' canarywoman" trucker who uses her feminine wiles on the dispatcher, to the "shoat-and-goat jockey" hauling livestock, or the "truck-stop commando" in the fancy rig.

Here he comes. You see him in the rear-view mirror of your Volkswagen. As he passes you, you know you better hang tight to your steering wheel. You've been watching that rig creep up on you for the last mile, its Christmas tree lights making it stand out like the aurora borealis against the night sky. The signposts say "Los Angeles—25 miles." But you know for sure you're in California because of the rigs passing you left and right. They're California trucks. There are two schools of thought about them: the Californians, who think that they are the finest in the world, and the rest of the country's truckers, who see them with the disdain born of jealousy.

52

Mighty Moe
El Paso, Texas

With the exception of Texas, California boasts the largest truck population in the country. Maybe it's the bad roads or the length of time it takes to get around, but many a West Coast gearjammer will spend as much time fixing up his rig as he will driving it. The essentials of a California truck include a big engine, an extra-long wheelbase, and some mighty good brakes. Something that will get you up those hills fast, and catch you going down roads like the California Grapevine. After the basics, the rest is all gravy. On the sides are the "West Coast mirrors," and the small convex "Volkswagen spotters." Large and rectangular in shape, the West Coast mirrors function like a cat's whiskers. If the mirrors can make it through, so can the rest of the rig.

Joe from Oakland has been driving the West Coast for a long time. When asked about the special conditions offered by the California terrain, he'll tell you quite frankly, "Buddy, they don't call those little white pills 'West Coast turnarounds' for nothing. If you can't stay awake, you're a dead man."

The lights on a California truck will surely keep you awake if the pills won't. The radiator grill of many a semi is hung with strands of Christmas lights in the shape of the driver's initials. Incandescent advertisements for themselves, they carve out a part of the darkness on the road ahead. Most West Coast rigs have "budd wheels" with a solid center instead of the usual spokes, and five, six, eight, or ten holes around the periphery. These are perfect for holding red, white, or blue lights inside the hubs to create a whirling psychedelic light show. That leaves the top of the cab to decorate. First come the long, silver bugles for the air horn, then the "torpedoes," the large, bullet-shaped clearance lights called, not surprisingly, California lights.

Joe's rig, like so many whose birthplace is the far side of the country, is a blaze of fire as it rolls down the highway. It's a double-bottomed trailer, two trailers hooked together cutting an eighty-foot-long path between the ocean and the Rockies. Eight hundred miles away from Joe's blazing rig, a trucker sits drinking a cup of muddy grounds in a small truck stop in Nevada, his accent as flat as the land he drives. "I don't think much of those truck-stop commandos. They spend all their time polishing chrome, instead of meeting broads. I think that's fishy." Call them truck-stop commandos or truckologists or even cowboys—it's a trucker's put-down, and reveals a natural distrust for anyone who spends too long primping or pomading his little corner of the world. A West Coast driver will tell you that no one else could haul those double-bottom rigs, or even triples with his consummate grace and being more of a trucker than most gives him license to put a little extra chrome or paint wherever he wants. After all,

does anyone call Muhammad Ali a flit for wearing satin trunks?

Down around the southern tip of California, near the Tijuana border, the trucks take on a Latin flavor. Mostly short-haulers driven by Mexican-Americans, they are painted in shades of turquoise-nugget blue and flesh pink. Their cabs are encrusted with small icons of the Holy Family and little skulls of lacquered bread are hung from the mirrors along with bright balls of fuzzy yarn.

Up north, heading towards the ragged chill of the Pacific Northwest, it's all business. The driver's seats are often covered by thick pelts of lamb's wool, and the truck's trailer swathed in extra-heavy tarps. Every truck has a supply of "mothballs," small round pellets of ether used to start a sluggish engine on an icy morning.

From the middle of California a man can cut straight across into Nevada in his crème de la crème of trucks, that brainchild of the Krazy Kalifornia Kulture of Kustomizing which has molded the amorphous dream of freedom and the open road into a tangible piece of steel and power. Drive that rolling palace right up to the Bronco Corral or another legal whorehouse, or maybe to the gambling tables, but drive there fast. The governor on the truck is probably set as high as it can go, and Nevada speeding tickets are few and far between as the El Dorados and Lincolns buzzing past wide open bear witness. In Las Vegas even the truck stops have one-armed bandits to help you lose your money, and the town is open twenty-four hours a day. Cruising in a forty-foot-long leopard-skin glory wagon is the best way to crash the dream city.

There are trucks that will flatter you, and there are trucks that will fool you. There are the "joners," the black-magic jinxed ones that will kill you in twenty different ways. And there are the pussycats, good for two or three million miles. Trucks also reflect the personality of the men who drive them. Strange, bigger than life, they never stay long enough in one place to be seen with a clear eye. Their statement is the roar of the air they displace when they roll by you on the road, or the empty spot next to you in the bed when a truck has taken your man away again. A man and his truck, a horse and his rider, a sailor and his ship, a hobo and his train—a relentless song of leaving and coming with never an end or beginning.

The wind is slowly dying down on those broad plains in Nebraska. The wheatfields are rippling gently and the dark night sky is being pushed back to make room for the dawn. The swollen eyes of the man at the wheel see, as he has seen countless times before, the lights of the city coming into view. He knows he will be able to stop and rest for a while before he must head on.

Roland

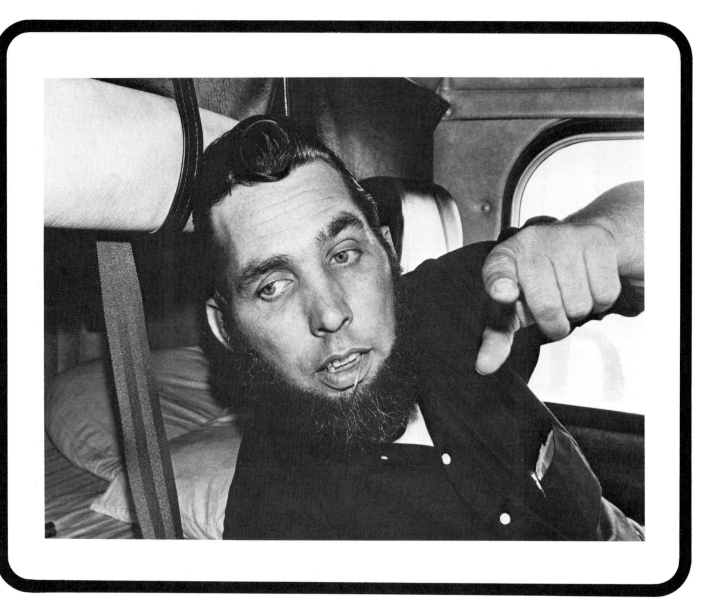

Before Roland rode trucks he rode Brahma bulls in the rodeo. It was on the rodeo circuit he picked up the habit of drinking fresh blood. Roland's first job was as a cowboy down in Florida, which, he will tell you, is the largest state for its size in the country. When a cow was slaughtered, Roland and his fellow wranglers would line up with their tin cups to catch the warm blood as it poured from the neck of the dying animal. The cowboys claim they drank the blood for strength and nourishment.

At six feet five, 290 pounds, Roland takes up a lot of space. His truck, a showroom-perfect 1974 Diamond Reo Cabover with an eight-foot-wide cab, just about gives him room to stretch. The rig is first-class all the way. Roland has a few homes around the country, but he spends practically all his time in the truck. He often says if he could he would find a woman to cook for him and be his companion and install a stove in the truck and never stop driving.

As it is, Roland, like most truckdrivers, has a wife, or in his case an ex-wife, tucked away somewhere. He also has a few kids and he loves them even though he's not quite sure if they're really his. The only thing Roland is uncomfortable talking about is his father. He left his mother when Roland was very young and Roland grew up living up to the vague memories he had about him. Like many boys in the South, Roland got married when he turned twenty-one. He hated marriage, but says that in the fifties, you just did it to be like everyone else.

In addition to truckdriving and Brahma bull riding, Roland's occupations, which he has a wallet full of union cards to prove, include heavy machinery mechanic, steelworker, and cosmetic salesman. A large suitcase of mink oil cosmetics is kept in the luggage compartment of his rig. Roland, with his massive arms, black beard, and ever-present toothpick, sells mink oil perfume and other dainties in whorehouses all over the country.

Roland grew his beard because he got angry whenever he went into a bar and saw the good-looking chicks going off with the "hippy types." He considers his beard a lucky charm and his "secret sex technique" is to rub it all over a woman until she is crawling the walls of his truck. Roland likes his sex straight without any "rigor mortis" (rigmarole). He grew up as a razor-toting redneck who fought his way through his teenage years in Florida. "There wasn't much to do on a Saturday night in Orlando 'cept hunt nigras an' alligators and brawl," says Roland, "and keep your wick well-lit with plenty of Rebel Yell bourbon." Roland pulls no

punches about his sexual proclivities. He'll tell you right off that, like most truckers, he's a very horny guy. He is proud of the fact that he is always "ripe and ready," but he will also look you in the eye and let you know another driver will do nicely if "there ain't no broads around." This is a fact of life on the road, and nothing that he feels ashamed about.

Roland is a collector of experiences. He once found himself in a roadshow production of *Lil' Abner*. He heard the pay was good, and didn't mind learning the song and dance numbers. Playing the part of Lil' Abner was like old times in Orlando. Wildcatting as an owner-operator, he follows his whims as they strike him. Picking up with a traveling carnival he drives a forty-foot reefer van with a frozen whale in it. Hauling the behemoth down the main street of town, Roland leans back in his cab. His white straw cowboy hat is tilted back on his head, his zippered boots opened wide to accommodate his heavy ankles and the toothpick is in place as he waves regally to the crowds of kids lining the way.

If Roland is coming over for dinner, don't expect any leftovers. A home-cooked meal is special for him, and he takes full advantage of one when he can. A four-pound leg of lamb or a "mutton" as he calls it is easily consumed along with two large baked sweet potatoes, carrots, beans, applesauce, five slabs of cornbread, apple pie, ice cream, and coffee. The meal is satisfactory, but a little foreign for Roland's down-home taste. The mountain oysters (skinned bull's balls), tripe, pigs' feet, and greens that he was raised on are more to his liking.

Like any veteran trucker, Roland is haunted by the specter of accidents, the gory details of which are a mainstay of conversation. His favorite story is about his own jackknife. He was driving in a rainstorm on the shifting red clay banks of Georgia where a trucker's brakes are useless. The huge loaded trailer "just walked around" and hit him broadside, causing thousands of dollars in damages to the cab, but none to him. Roland was lucky to escape unhurt, but he has been on the road too long to believe it won't happen again. He faces the possibility of death every day. Every bad curve or icy road leaves its mark and narrows the odds. "I'd rather die on the road than live off it," he says as his clear blue eyes catch snakes and rabbits running across the road too fast for a non-trucker to see. "There's nothing out there for me...there never was ...I'd rather ride this truck for one more year than live for fifty in one place." Roland replaces his toothpick with a fresh one.

57

Old Sam

Old Sam is mad. It's his first run in his new rig and it's sitting in the lube bay of a Union 76, flat-out broken. Sam is resting on the rim of a discarded tire, cracking his knuckles as he curses out that bitch of a truck. What it is, is downright embarrassing. Gypsies, wildcatters, and cowboys are all lined up on the exit ramp fueled up and ready to go and Sam, as righteous a trucker as you could find, sits there with a busted axle.

It's been Sam's dream to finally get a loan to buy this semi, $45,000 worth of roll-and-tuck upholstery, chrome fittings, quadraphonic stereo, CB radio, carpeting, a custom console, and two long chrome stacks billowing thick black diesel smoke behind. No more crummy dog trucks for this gearjammer. After thirty years on the road Sam had driven them all and was ready for the best—the Rolls-Royce of trucks—a Kenworth. No more Macks with that bulldog growl between gears, no more Whites with the nuts and bolts popping out after every bump, and nothing in between. Sam wanted the best money could buy. He picked her up himself, straight from the factory, and as he drove her away he noticed the blank spaces on the odometer, and imagined how he would put so many miles on this truck that he would spin her all the way back to zero again.

His first stop with the new truck was Dan's custom paint shop in Texarkana. Sam and Mike spent a few hours going over ideas for custom paint jobs. Sam wanted leopard spots and a tail curling out the back with the words "tiger in my tank" painted on the side. Mike thought that a roadrunner was more the ticket, but Sam accused him of being too lazy to do the spots. After throwing out Casper the Friendly Ghost, women in a kaleidoscope of poses, dice, beer bottles, Rebel flags, pinstriping, his mother's name, and a big map of Arkansas, they finally hit on it. Sam doesn't remember exactly whose idea it was or what exactly it was about but he knew it was right. Directly above each headlamp against the midnight blue of the rig's body Dan painted two hands. In the palm of each was a flame. People asked Sam what those hands meant, and he would answer them depending on his mood. Sometimes he would give them a biblical quote, sometimes a story about burning his palm on another man's woman, and sometimes he would tell them to mind their own business.

Sitting in the lube bay isn't exactly Sam's idea of what owning the new rig would be like. He had heard too many stories about eighteen-year-old hitchhikers, who were naked under their London Fog raincoats, and lonely housewives who hung out at truck stops, to rest easy hanging around the parking lot. He somehow always thought it was his beat-up truck with the paint chipping off, and the interior that looked like an old sock that kept the women away. Sometimes he would catch a glance of himself in a rest-room mirror, and could not help but notice that all the Schlitz had finally taken its toll. He knew he was outclassed by the young studs who would spend two hundred dollars on a pair of custom cowboy boots. Sometimes another trucker would tell him he was old-fashioned. He still wore his shirt sleeves down flat instead of rolled up and hugging his biceps, showing off the lumps of muscle that develop with the constant shifting of gears. He still called his wallet a "chain-drive pocketbook," recalling the old days when a man's wallet often disappeared in a roadside bunkhouse. Of course, he was a little jealous of these new road boys, but he knew he was every bit the trucker they were, and then some. He remembered way back before the California Grapevine was fully paved, and he knew the names of all the waitresses from Oregon to Arkansas.

The "maniac," Sam's favorite term for mechanic, was finishing up his rig now. It was under warranty, and the job wouldn't cost him a cent, but it was the principle of the damn thing. The mechanic gave Sam the five-minute sign. Just enough time for one more cup of "hundred-mile coffee."

Sam got up off the old tire and headed for the cafeteria of the truck stop. The tile in the rest room echoed his footsteps and he caught a reflection of himself multiplied many times over. He washed his face and rolled his sleeves a little; just enough to notice that his arms were in pretty fine shape. After all, he had been on the road for thirty years, and that was his big baby Kenworth outside waiting for him.

He walked to the coffee counter lined with other drivers all drinking coffee and playing the jukebox. Sam sat down next to a young driver, offhandedly asking him which rig he belonged to, knowing full well the question would be returned.

58

3

His Loves

As I topped a rising hill
And reached a telephone
I dialed seven digits cross the land
To reach my little home.

After the dinner dishes are put away and the babysitter plans have been confirmed, Loretta Haneley steps into the shower stall, carefully making sure to step squarely on the swan-shaped safety-skid appliques lining the tile floor. Her Lady Gillette razor slices up the length of her leg cutting the throats of any newly sprouted stubble. After two separate soapings with Vitabath Pink the old flutter in her stomach begins. It starts slowly, tracing up her arms and tingling along the nape of her neck, at precisely the point where her roots need retouching the most. It revives the memory of her last night out, a week ago. The anticipation is savored until it is replaced by the guilt that shifts her thoughts to her truckdriving husband.

Loretta's mother warned her about truckdrivers and traveling salesmen. She told her what went on at those lonely truck stops so far from a wife's watchful eye. It seemed all her life Loretta had heard stories about the waitresses and lonely housewives who flashed their smiles and rolled their hips at men like her husband.

The hot water from the antiquated furnace had run out again leaving a trail of iridescent bubbles sliding down her back. As Loretta steps into the striped bathtowel, she hears the ringing of the telephone. Trailing baby powder she rushes toward the bedroom. The voice on the other end is familiar and would ordinarily be comforting, but not on Thursday night. Stan, her husband, always did have bad timing. Loretta flashes on the memory of her mother taking her to the hospital when the labor pains started in lieu of her husband who was late with his run.

Stan is spending the night in Nevada, 1800 miles from home. In a flat voice he describes the long haul he is on, the lousy truck the company has given him, the blowout on the rear recap, and the bitter coffee that is burning a hole in his gut.

Loretta listens patiently…kiss kiss…I love you, too…so do the kids…drive carefully…and it's all over. Stan's voice is replaced by a hollow buzzing and then nothing. Loretta sits on the edge of the bed, eyes half-focused on the French provincial dresser with the alarm clock on top. Slowly she starts to roll on her panty hose one leg at a time, trying hard to force the guilt down to acceptable levels. She would never give her mother the satisfaction of being right. No matter how bad she felt sleeping in a half-filled double bed. Thursday had become her safety valve, her night out that kept her sane the rest of the week.

Loretta finishes dressing and slips on her coat as she disappears through the door heading for the local truck stop; 1800 miles away her husband's tired eyes have come to rest on the nervously tapping foot of a woman sitting alone at the truck-stop counter. She smiles, and nodding his head he moves toward her.

Womans Lib is alright I guess
For those who want to play the part
But I've always thought myself
It takes two mules to pull my cart.

As Mary slips the wedding ring from her finger she notices the indented red circle it has left on her finger. Mary lives in Cairo, Illinois. She has been married to Jim, a steel hauler, for ten years. Her marriage to Jim has always been a good one. It came as quite a shock when she found out she wasn't Jim's only wife.

Sure, she had heard all the truckdrivin' songs and stories about the gearjammer with the six wives, and the one about the long-hauler who married the same woman five times, but she figured that like most trucker's stories they were two parts diesel smoke and one part bullshit.

Mary started to get suspicious when a letter was forwarded to her from the terminal dispatcher. It was addressed to a Mrs. James Peterson, but when she opened it she knew she didn't have a charge account at Macy's in Albany, New York. Things started to fall together like rocks in an avalanche, and a quick call to the Albany operator produced the other Mrs. James Peterson, wife of a midwestern trucker.

At first Mary found it all so outrageous it made her laugh. She almost had to admire Jim, who had always seemed so shy and awkward around women. But as she spoke to the other woman on the phone, and heard what she thought to be children's voices in the background, she felt a sick dull pain in her stomach that started to throb, and she no longer knew what to do If it had been an affair she could have dealt with it: she had read enough issues of *Cosmopolitan* all slick and shiny, waiting seductively each month in her post-office box, to know how to handle an affair, but she had never seen a solution to a problem like hers.

The other woman had been married to Jim for five years, and together they had produced two sons. Mary envied her. The daughters she had given Jim had always been a sore point between them. Too late Mary realized that she must have been imagining his bad feelings all these years, since Jim already had all the sons a man could want. In all the years of their marriage Jim had never told Mary what his salary was. They seemed to live more sparsely than most of the other trucker families they knew, but she always figured that he must have been socking the money away for their old age, or college for the children, so she never complained.

Now she wondered what she would say to Jim when he came home. She had just placed the receiver of the old black phone in its cradle cutting off the loud sobs of the other woman. Jim was on the road and Mary knew that it would be at least two weeks until she would be able to confront him with her discovery. Mary wondered whom he would choose, the woman from Albany, whose dress was a size seven according to the bill she had just received, or her, whose dress size had long ago reached two digits. Could the other woman cook a peach tart as well as she could? After all it was Jim's favorite—or was it? Did she make love differently?

What kind of sheets did they sleep on? All the horrid questions as painful and common as adultery filled her head like a thick dull smoke. The worst fear, the most terrifying idea was the possibility that she and the woman from Albany were not the last of Jim Peterson's wives.

Mary went shopping, as she had always done all her life when she was upset. The order and grandeur of the department store helped to ease her own confusion. She bought a new dress, a slip with fresh white straps. She didn't worry about pinching pennies for their future. When she returned home Mary relined the dresser drawers with perfumed paper festooned with violets scattered in a baroque design.

Three weeks passed and Jim was due home soon. She sent her daughters to sleep over at a neighbor's house and she waited, hands folded tensely on her lap for Jim to arrive.

That's a mighty fearsome-looking rig
Until you climb inside
And you're not near as big a man
As I had you in my mind.

Roscoe is an ex-Marine. He has two kids, three ex-wives and a picture of Raquel Welch in a doeskin bikini taped up over the bunk in the sleeper box of his truck. The tattoo on his left bicep is a Marine bulldog in a combat helmet and the words "hot" and "cold" are tattooed in flowing script over his nipples. Roscoe is the half owner of a brand-new $35,000 tractor trailer. His partner "Doc," standing 6 feet 2 inches and tipping in at 210 pounds, is every bit as tough as Roscoe. Roscoe and Doc have been driving together for five years. It was a lonely night in a truck stop outside of Baltimore when they became lovers. Doc was the aggressor. Roscoe had done a little "buddy fuckin'" in the Marines, but as he put it, "It's a little habit I picked up in the service to alleviate the boredom, and anyway, what the hell, a hole's a hole." Roscoe hates to talk about the details of his affair with Doc. He still insists that he prefers women and both he and Doc have an agreement about the other men they want. Although Roscoe operates with the subtlety of a bull moose in his daily work, when it comes to his other homosexual encounters he uses an elaborate vocabulary of signals.

A lingering glance over the urinal wall, or the flexing of an ass cheek in the shower stall speaks volumes. Although there is a queen-size sleeper in their truck, Doc and Roscoe alternate sleeping at the truck-stop motel, allowing each other to use the truck for their "dates." Both men know the awful loneliness that trucking brings on and the pure pleasure of another warm body close to yours in an anonymous truck lot. They also understand each other's need for independence. They offer each other no ties that bind. The feeling of being trapped is what put them on the road in the first place. Roscoe and Doc deal only with other truckers. They like tall studs with long thighs and low-slung jeans, and a pair of slick boots doesn't hurt. They both hate the "faggots" who knock on their truck door at night looking for action.

Petie is one young piece of flesh who will never find his way into Roscoe's sleeper cab. Petie used to work around the meat district on One Hundred Twenty-fifth Street in New York City. He is eighteen and has been turning tricks since he can remember. He always hated school and he was poor and it seemed like a good way to make money.

One of his friends told him about a truckdriver who would park his truck on the west side of town near the river, and for a quick blowjob and a percentage would let the local hookers turn tricks in his truck trailer. The small purple scar running along the side of Petie's head was carved into his future the first time he tried to hustle. He was the "chicken" for middle-aged trucking "hawks" marooned on the docks of the city. He remembers that he wore his extra-tight Banlon shirt that night and high-waisted pants. Four-inch platforms and a sprinkling of glitter in his peroxided hair completed the outfit. The glitter was a steal from Mama Red, the most notorious queen in the district, but Mama Red was getting old and ugly, and Petie was young blood for the streets to suck dry. The truckdriver he first serviced that night was on the downhill side of a two-week bennie run. He couldn't get an erection no matter how hard Petie worked him over, so out came a knife, and carved its way up Petie's smooth bronze cheek.

He will admit that his clients are rougher than most. That they use him with a vengeance until he feels like the sides of beef swinging over his head. The toes of his glitter specked platform shoes strain to anchor him among the pieces of fat and scrap meat on the trailer's floor.

Eventually Petie will move to New Jersey where he will work the rest stops on the highway, and the "gay

truckers only" clubs. He will escape the rivalry of Mama Red and the dangers of the New York docks, and be as settled down and domesticated as his lifestyle will ever allow.

For she was soft as satin
With a heart as pure as gold
But your mighty roar lured me on
And claimed my very soul.

Not all truck-stop hookers work out of the back of a truck. Most truckdrivers are welcome in civilian whorehouses. But a non-trucker is persona non grata in trucker territory. The trucker-only whorehouses exist all over the country but seem to proliferate in the south. In the heart of South Carolina there is a strip of road running perpendicular to the Interstate that is crowded with small buildings that look like gas stations but sell a different type of energy. They all have signs in the window with the warning "truckers only" and the invitation for "free coffee." The foolish few who enter the premises looking for coffee or gas or those who can't produce an ICC card will be hustled out at supersonic speed.

The small cubicles lining the corridors and the camper out back are filled with women waiting to relieve the tensions of the road. The women, like the road their customers travel, seem bleak and weary and as tacky as the pink and white awnings outside advertising "love gas." A platinum-wigged face peeks out from behind the curtains, a face that doesn't see the light of day much—or maybe its chalkiness is the result of layers of "Ivory Blush" foundation punctuated with pale lipstick. As cliqueish as their clientele, these roadside madonnas carefully adopt the "good girl gone wrong" image, exactly the type of female who has inspired the whining twanging songs of the country-western singer. The price for their services is around twenty-five dollars for a blowjob or fifty dollars for a half-and-half (intercourse and a blowjob with a half-hour limit). Of course the rates vary with the reputation of the woman, a "cajun queen" or a young "nymphet" will bring more money than most, and of course tips are always in order.

If the cost of a truck-stop whore seems surprisingly high for the style of the services rendered, it should be remembered that life on the road is expensive, and the

A truck-stop hooker

truckdriver, limited by his rig and his habits, pays through the nose for his bread and butter as well as his gravy.

There is a steady stream of customers in the little roadstops, but the heavy activity is at night, when even the local sheriff checks out the action and pockets his share of the day's take. The tiny, South Carolina palaces have none of the sophisticated trappings of their northern equivalent. There are no massage tables or sunken bubble baths, no exotic rubbing oils scented with lemon Zest or patchouli. It is plain and simple sex…the truckdrivers prefer it like that.

Of course there is always the threat of the clap. When a truck-stop cutie swings by in her white vinyl boots and laced up hot pants, a man's better judgment often leaves him. There are about as many "surefire" ways of detecting the clap as there are truck stops. Canadian Joker, a gearjammer from the northern provinces always carries a twenty-dollar bill with a picture of the Queen on it in his chain-drive pocketbook. Eyes twinkling, he says, "If the queen turns up her nose it's a bad sign. Billy J. who has been hauling wildcat loads for the last twelve years has a more scientific test. He puts a copper penny stuck to a wad of bubble gum on his index finger. His index finger with the gum and penny ease their way into a woman's crotch, and then Billy waits for the results. If she doesn't notice, she's clean. If she screams from irritation of the copper— forget it! The system is rather like the princess and the pea in reverse.

64

There's a woman down in Macon
Waiting there for me
And this diesel's always got a spot
Under a big oak tree.

Jack knows all about the cat houses down south. He has been driving the highways for most of his working life and he is not naive. But all his money and most of his time not spent on the road is spent at home with his wife and two sons. The money that he earns is patiently budgeted to provide for food, rent, clothes and an occasional trip to a religious retreat. A little money is always laid aside for the toy trucks which Jack builds for his sons. He has created a small fleet of trucks handcrafted from wood and scrap metal, and complete with miniature gearshifts, odometers, mirrors, and enough lights to make any little child happy. The trucks are models of the Macks, Kenworths, and Peterbilts that Jack drives every day.

Jack and his wife live in a small southern town in a white house that sits in the shadow of their landlord's larger house. The furniture is old and there are no fancy carpets or objets d'art that would define a more affluent lifestyle. Displayed on the coffee table is Jack's prize possession, a large Bible with colorful illustrations that bring to mind a Charlton Heston epic. There is a blond wood television in the corner of the room and a homemade collage of a truck hanging above it. On the stove is a berry pie, made by Jack's wife Pat, a large pale woman in her twenties with a face like a harvest moon.

The youngest son, age three, is sleeping face down in his parents' double bed. The house has a very faint smell of urine but is as clean and inviting as dedicated care can make it. The afternoon sun filters through the drawn venetian blinds tempering the scorching August heat. Trucks dominate the decor. There are truck pictures, truck toys, and truck poems all handwritten and neatly filed away in notebooks by Jack. Pat doesn't worry about her sons playing truckdriver or about her husband's plans to take them on trips in his truck when they are older. She knows Jack isn't like the other men she hears stories about. Jack's main problem is that the other truckdrivers don't think he is a trucker. They see only his delicate face and slender body that belie his obsession with the road and travel. The singing of his eighteen-wheeler is like a muse's harp. Jack doesn't tell many people about his poetry or his religion but prefers to sit in a back booth of the local truck stop listening to Tom T. Hall on the jukebox for inspiration.

When his haul is over he will come home for berry pies, and to the tin clubhouse in the back yard where his sons spend the sultry afternoons searching for bears or glovin' the old softball. Soon he will start work on the latest truck for them, his hands skillfully molding the lines of his children's legacy.

**A trucking family
Branford, Connecticut**

65

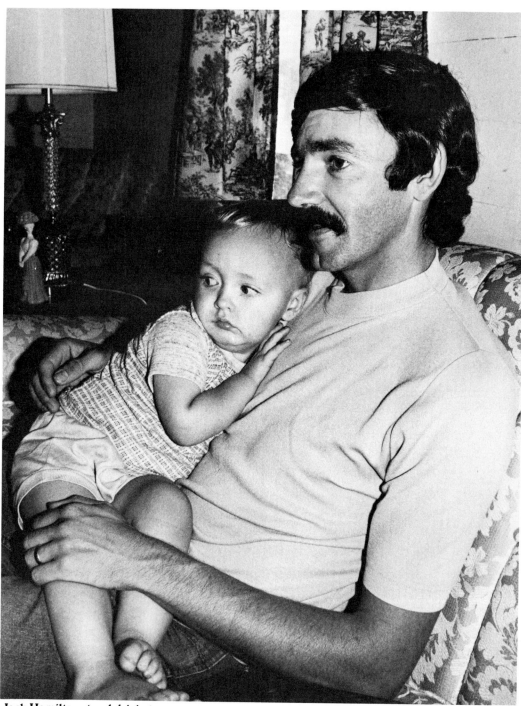

Jack Hamilton, truckdriving poet

A trucker's sons at play

When Daddy's gone far from home
And day's end comes creeping by
I sit in the shade of his favorite tree
And wonder is he thinking of me?

Fuel stops, road blocks, sleeper cab dreams
License checks, loading docks, truck-stop queens
Weighing in, weighing out, filling out the log
To be a truly trucker, you have to love it all.

Somewhere in the midwest a fourth-grade teacher is sending a note home to a troubled parent. The note will be received by Lorinda Spratt, a truckdriver's wife. The note concerns the fact that Mrs. Spratt's son Michael draws trucks all day long. His arithmetic suffers, his notebooks suffer, and today Mrs. Spratt is at her wit's end. She told her best friend Ruth that the last straw was when the teacher told her of the spidery outline of a truck scratched into the wall of the classroom.

Last year her husband took Michael on a few short runs in the truck, an old LJ Mack. He let Michael sit in the driver's seat and turn the giant wheel while he looked over the snub-nosed hood. He showed Michael how to shift the gears and what the clutch did and the two of them rode together like driver and shotgun. They watched the countryside sail by the window. When night came Michael slept in the sleeper bunk with his father, and in the morning shared coffee-spiked milk with his father at the truck stop. Michael came back from the trip wearing a visored cap with a Mack Bulldog on it. He wore it around the house, and he wore it at play, and then he started wearing it to school. When Michael's teacher made him take off the cap he started to draw trucks.

Mrs. Spratt of Gary, Indiana, has been a trucker's wife too long to let the little drawings pass unnoticed. She has seen other mothers' sons get the fever and long ago she made up her mind that her son would not grow up to drive a truck. She knows how it burns a man out too quickly. The life is too hard, and the rewards too meager. She has seen the heavy lines etching into her husband's face long before their time, and she was worried about the ulcer he has been developing over the years. Everything had been fine until those little drawings appeared. Mrs. Spratt will write the school telling them she will stop the drawings, but she knows better. All the reprimands, all the broken pencils in the world can't make a boy forget that up-high flyin' feeling that his daddy loves.

Princess has just finished her act and is struggling into her old pink cardigan. Her nipples, which have been sprayed with a freezing solution to keep them erect, are pushing against the nappy material. Princess has told her boss at the Club 69 where she is an "exotic" dancer that he better turn up the heat or she will quit. The boss insists that his customers, who are truckdrivers, won't drink as much if the heat is too high.

The club that Princess works, like the truckers-only whorehouses, is open only to trucking men. The acts are fairly routine striptease numbers and the girls strip all the way but don't show "split beaver" as her boss calls it. The strippers range from good-looking to downright ugly. Princess, one of the best-looking, is the club's headliner. She has been an "exotic" for three years now. Before she joined the Club 69 she was married to a truckdriver, learned to drive a rig, and even seriously thought of getting a truck of her own. She occasionally travels to other clubs on the underground truck circuit, but she shies away from performing for non-truckers.

She is sitting in her dressing room taking off her makeup and talking about her marriage. Behind her is the little velvet stool she uses in her act when she unrolls her net stockings. She has written the name "Princess" on it with a tube of glue and then sprinkled glitter over the lettering. Princess feels it adds a touch of class to her act. She is extremely sensitive to appearing "cheap." When her husband found out she was dancing in a club he called her a "hoor" and a slut, and she has never forgotten the sting of those words. Princess had married at a young age. It was the kind of marriage that happens in a too-large family where marriage offered more space and a little more food for hungry mouths. Her husband was twenty-five years her senior. "I still love him in a way, but I wouldn't go back to him," she will tell you. "I like men lookin' at me, admiring me, and I didn't want to just sit home and wait for him to come to me."

69

Truckdriver and daughter
Monroe, North Carolina

Princess was raised in West Virginia, not far from the Club 69. Being part Indian accounts for her broad cheekbones and tawny complexion, and she is often billed as a Polynesian, which gets her a lot closer to "class" then being a half-Indian coal miner's daughter.

The most satisfying sexual experience that Princess can recall is when she made love in the back of an old Freightliner with a trucker she knew. She was aware that his co-driver could hear every moan and sigh and this turned her jet higher and higher until she exploded in a crescendo of eye-rolling, lip-biting passion.

Princess wants to change her act. She thinks she will buy an air seat from a truck and wear cowboy boots and a ten-gallon hat. She wants to practice with a lariat which she could use to throw out into the audience and lasso compliant truckers into assisting her on stage. "I guess the most disappointing thing that happened to me since I started dancing is that the drivers don't talk to me after the show," she says. Princess finishes adjusting her false eyelashes by tapping them down in the corners with a long labia-pink enameled fingernail. Then her hands flutter like tawny birds over her dressing table and dart and swoop into the heaps of Blush-on, gels, encapsulated moisture creams, placenta-based lipsticks, and two varieties of musk oil douche powder.

She turns quickly as the door opens and a strange man peeks in. The door snaps shut and she pouts. "See what I mean—they're all scared of me." The eyelash pops again. "I'm number five on the list—first trucks, then their wives, then the kids, and the coffee...I get whatever is left."

Princess hears the opening notes of her taped intro-duction, the first bars of the funky "Night Train." She adjusts her silver pants suit with the tricky zippers and, pushing her slender feet into her spike heels, she edges her way towards the door of the dressing room. To me, or to herself, or maybe to no one in par-ticular she says, "Hell, maybe an airhorn would help, too, and a tire billy," and disappears into a raucous cheering that fades as the door closes.

When the highway stretches out
And all life seems to go
She comes to ride beside me
And keep me on the road.

Pull into any truck stop after dark and chances are the stories are being hung out like wash on a line. There is the one about the jackknife on some icy road, or the one about the truck flattening the old farmer's barn. The most popular stories of all are the ones about the hitchhiking women. The stories sing of balls and glory and women cruising the nation's high-ways nude under flimsy raincoats. Somewhere there may be a woman hitchhiking around the country clad in little more than black lace panties, but she must be close to eighty and have traveled at least 30,000 miles a week to have ridden with all the truckers who have picked her up.

Hank has sat in this particular booth many times. He knows the mottled formica as well as he knows the wallpaper in his wife's kitchen, maybe better. The story he is telling is his favorite.

It is the one about the "honest-to-God nymphomaniac" that he picked up outside of Toledo. According to Hank's gospel the girl removed her black satin bikini panties and draped them over the gearshift knob of his truck. Sometimes if the audience is receptive Hank will embellish the story with more detail. The mystery woman will have on nylons and a garter belt. Sometimes hot pants with crotchless panties. The phrases that burst from her ripe lips sound suspi-ciously like the dialogue in the plain-cover novels tucked into the glove compartment of his truck.

What Hank won't tell his friends is the true story of what happened to him last June in Billings, Montana. As he was rolling down the Interstate he spotted a blonde thumbing a ride. He was firing up six inches of Carolina stogie when he pulled his truck to a dead halt at her feet. Five minutes after she settled into the shotgun seat she unbuttoned her blouse and threw it out the window. At first Hank couldn't believe his eyes. It was as if all the stories he had ever told had suddenly come true. But then she hit him with the con: fifty dollars or she would jump out at the next toll station and scream rape. It was the oldest road con around and Hank knew better than to challenge her and lose his job. He gave her the money and held his anger inside. He pulled over and let her out of the truck watching as she quickly pulled a spare blouse from her oversized purse and slipped it on. When he looked in the rearview mirror he could see her posed by the side of the road. Tonight is different for Hank— he is among friends and the stories about good women and impossible dreams are recited, fondled a bit sadly, and passed along with love to the next guy.

My heart had beat a million times
For a love I thought was true
But that was long before my eyes
Came to fall on you.

Jerry is posing for me. He has stripped down to the nylon underwear which rides up the crack in his ass and hangs low under his beer gut. The Jerry Lewis telethon is on TV and a bottle of Old Grand Dad sits half empty by the "magic fingers" bed. Jerry is a truckdriver and an exhibitionist. He likes to drive the highways in Canada, the ones that are long stretches of endless road, wearing nothing but his underpants and cowboy boots. Jerry is also a reader of "swingers magazines," and as an owner-operator he schedules his loads to the geographical requirements of his sex life. By his side, on the truck's "dogbox" is his Polaroid camera. It is an old model and he is not completely

satisfied with it, planning to trade it in on an SX 70. The pictures that he takes are mainly of himself. He asks friends to photograph him in different stages of nudity, starting fully dressed in the gray sharkskin suit he picked up for fifty dollars in Texas, and ending in the nude. The suit is way too long in the arms and legs, and is worn strictly for posing with a frilled shirt and a western tie. He wears his buckskin "split-shifting" gloves on his hands and poses with a range of expressions that move from neo–Winston Churchill to childlike amazement at the discovery of his own flesh.

Jerry is twenty-eight. But you'd never take him for a day under forty-five. The lines around his eyes and the bloat of his body is contradicted only by the not-quite-formed expression on his face. He can tell you a hundred stories about the road, about the waitresses in Ontario who serve themselves up to truckers with the rolls and coffee. He will tell you about the ones who use alum to tighten themselves, often asking truckers to hold their douche bags for them. Jerry is a leg man. When asked if he prefers blondes to brunettes he will tell you that if it was hair he wanted to feel he would just reach up and palm his own. head. The truck stops he likes are the ones that deal in "pussy, pills, and coffee." The best memory of his driving days came last November when he was hauling a load of maple syrup through the provinces and was hailed by a woman and her teenage daughter stranded by the side of the road with a flat tire.

He pulled his rig over and explained to the woman that he would help her but he was only wearing his briefs since he liked to be "comfortable." Cold as it was he leaped from the cab to fix the woman's tire, but not before doing a snaky reverse striptease into his tight jeans and sweater. The woman and her daughter got a long look at the ritual dressing and the highpoint of the scene came when the woman muttered "well hung." Was that all? No passionate coupling in the truck, no ménage à trois of young mother, teenage daughter, and trucker? No, according to Jerry, just the memory of eyes searing into the crotch of his nylon pants, the same ones that are now obscuring Jerry Lewis from the color TV.

72

Jerry
Wheeling, West Virginia

I eased out on the highway
And found four forward gears
But missed the fifth for on my mind
Lingered one of Baby's tears.

"I'm much gentler than other guys…" Holly says it, Richard says it, and so do countless others. It is the ultimate trucker's line. The other used mostly but not necessarily with good-looking women is "I don't have any use for good-lookin' broads, they're usually lousy in the sack." The first line contradicts the hard nosed truckdrivers' image, while simultaneously calling attention to it. The second line advertises a coolness and worldliness designed to knock the wind out of a confident woman's sails.

Both are devastatingly effective, and, to ears that are used to the poetic and well-reasoned arguments of Ivy League seducers, the lines come as a surprise. The idea of a man *not* being gentle is a novelty these days with sensitivity training and male conciousness groups abounding. The roughness and naivete of the approach can be more effective that the most urbane and sophisticated panty-prying.

Holly, like most truckers who embrace the life completely, doesn't often pass the same way twice. Before he makes love to you he will tell you two things. The first is that God made man in his own image and woman second, and therefore not equal. Second, he will tell you that he will reroute his truck so he can see you more often. This will never happen and he will remain just a ghost of a memory on your body and your mind. Holly doesn't have the time to take good care of himself and he's missing quite a few teeth. The side ones are gone, making his already concave cheeks caress the bones even more intimately, but his front few are still intact and they look pretty good. He has black grease under his knuckles. The texture of his lips on yours is rough, from the wind and the road dirt blowing the oils and sweat from his face. He won't want any part of oral sex either—it's too perverse; only hippies do it—and because of his small penis he will often ask for a discount at the whorehouses he frequents.

Holly is sexy; logically he shouldn't be, but there's something undeniably refreshing about his "facts" of sex, and his simple demands in the face of today's cumbersome sophistication. When he enters you it won't be in one of the hundred and one positions of the Kama Sutra or Chapter 15 from *The Joy of Sex*. His loving is meat and potatoes instead of Julia Child, a country-western lament while Vivaldi and Bach sit in the corner with their lips pursed. When it's over and the bunk is filled with the smoke from a detumescent cigarette, the eagerness to move on is in Holly's eye. Try as you may to not see it, it is there and he will stretch his long frame and slip on his boots mumbling something about calling the next time he comes your way, but there won't be a next time and that is, in a way, the best part of all.

76

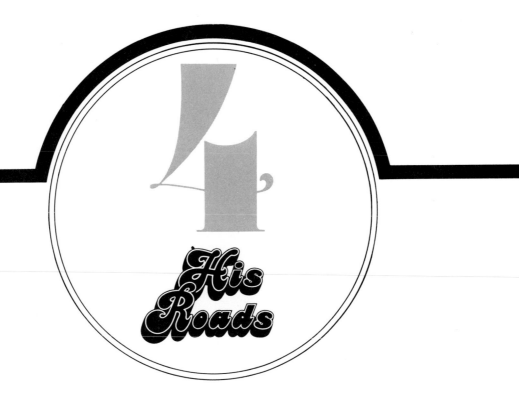

His Roads

Jack of Diamonds is bear hunting in the Monfort lane. He's got the hammer down on his eighteen-wheeler, and doesn't plan to slow down until he gets near that choke and puke outside Des Moines. Silos filled with corn line the charcoal gray ribbon of asphalt that is fast turning to ice. Jack of Diamonds says that truck-driving boils down to two words: "loads" and "roads." The loads are short-term problems. Whether they are hot or ill-paying or a nuisance like cows or refrigerated strawberries, you can dump them off at their destination and be on your way again. The roads, however, never change, and while they may one minute lull you with their long hypnotic vistas, the next minute they can send your truck spinning into oblivion.

Jack divides truckers into two types: the Monforts and the McLeans. The latter are those who plod along in the lane named after the utilitarian trucks of the McLean Company. The Monfort lane got its handle from the high-powered custom trucks, dubbed "circus wagons," that bear the name of the Monfort Beef Company. Whenever Jack of Diamonds hits the midwest, he takes advantage of its roads. "God must have made the midwest especially for truckers. I've done seventy miles an hour all the way through Nebraska, sleeping all the way, and never once had to make a turn."

A man's response to the roads he travels is always personal. The part of the country he calls his home has a lot to do with it. If he was raised in the Rocky Mountains, the majestic peaks will look a lot less frightening through the windshield than they will to a level-eyed midwesterner. A gearjammer driving in New England sees either nestling hills and rolling fields or a deathtrap of hairpin turns and icy roads.

Over the years, some roads have developed reputations as "killer highways"—places so bad that the very mention of their names raises the hair on the back of a trucker's neck. A litany of dangerous names and places is recited over steaming cups of coffee at cafes around the country—a chant for the many who didn't make the other side of the mountain.

Roads and weather conditions that keep the ordinary tourist home in front of the fireplace don't faze the truckdriver. It takes a mighty bad stretch of road to turn him around—one so bad his brakes catch fire, or his brake fluid ignites the whole underbelly of the truck, or a curve so sharp that there's just no way he can pull fifty-five feet and forty tons around it.

These stretches of asphalt nightmare are nicknamed with the dubious affection given hurricanes and other natural disasters. A driver approaching the California Grapevine better be prepared with a lot of driving know-how and maybe a few extra prayers. The Grapevine, lying due north of Los Angeles, is fifteen miles of steep continuous descent. The only thing between a runaway truck and the ragged face of the mountain is a meager line of sandbags, only recently added by the highway patrol. As you grind down the road, you hope that your brakes stay cool, and your cargo isn't flammable, and that you don't wind up like Frying Pan Fran. Fran had taken the wheel while her husband was sawing wood in the sleeper. Trying to pass a car full of slow-going senior citizens, she put the hammer down too far, and before she knew it the brakes ignited and she was hauling a load of fifty thousand pounds of barbecued cantaloupes. Her husband woke up just in time to see his flaming truck steered into the side of the mountain.

Second in infamy to the Grapevine is Fancy Gap in West Virginia. It lies in the shadow of that strange protuberance known as Mount Airy on Route 52 near the North Carolina border. Lining the approach are souvenir shacks selling Confederate flags and salty country hams. The road itself is a long, ear-popping climb of twisting, mountainous curves. The purple blue shadows of the steep cliffs and the chilled rustic air only add to the arcane danger. At the foot of the worst curve on Fancy Gap you can find Kate's house. Kate is a slight, gray-haired hillbilly woman whose front porch affords a panoramic view of the jackknifing rigs. Truckers call it "Kate's Curve" in acknowledgment of the many times Kate has called the state troopers to rescue a trucker who has landed, cab and trailer, on her front steps.

The roads are bad enough without the practical jokes played by bored and ornery people. Daniel Perpeet drives the Smokie Mountains frequently, and has a score of stories to tell about as many trips. "Once I was on old Route 77 comin' up from the Carolinas, when a bullet (I believe it was a 30-30) came through my windshield. I sure knew it wasn't a rock, 'cause it went straight through the shotgun seat. The troopers I called in to look at it finally traced it to a crazy old hillbilly set up there in the woods by the side of the road. He had heard tell of a truck shutdown where everybody was sniping at the truckdrivers and he throught he would get in on the action."

One of the most hazardous pranks is a favorite of children. Like producers of a down-home disaster movie, they glaze the black-topped roads with a layer of soap, either applied with giant cakes of laundry soap, or mixed from a box of detergent. The road becomes a two-lane skating rink, and the front wheels on contact start to skid and slide wildly as a hidden audience of childish eyes watch the giant truck fall from the road. Notorious among truckers are the citizens of a little border town on the Phoenix-California line who practically held town meetings to think of original ways to harass the road-weary drivers.

Any mountain pass is a hazard, and the Smokies are honeycombed with them. Claude's Mountain in Virginia, Old Flat Top, also in Virginia, Cabazon Pass, Black Mountain in Asheville, North Carolina, all mean trouble to truckers—especially in the winter when the snow starts to swirl, and the ice pellets fly with fury against the muffled radiator grills of the truck.

When spring thaws the road, and the blankets are unzipped from the radiator, and the chrome is lovingly repolished, life on the "boulevard" is renewed with an enthusiasm that crackles like lightning over the CB radios. On a good day like this, ask "End Table," a furniture mover who mostly works the midwest, where the bad roads in the heartland are. He will shrug his broad shoulders trying hard to remember a flaw on that perfect terrain. Mirroring the broad, flat accents of its inhabitants, the roads of the midwest are wide open and uncomplicated. Cutting a broad swatch across the center of the country, the main dangers of the high-

This Highway's Mean

This highway's mean and hateful
It tears a man apart
It takes him from the ones he loves
And breaks his very heart.

It crushes love with eighteen wheels
So could you tell me then
Why this road is loved so much
By so many lonely men?

80

ways of Iowa, Nebraska, and Illinois lie in becoming hypnotized by the perfect flatness of the land. A center strip of white seems to stretch on forever, creating a glassy mirror-like patina on the blacktop. There are few landmarks, endless acres of corn and other crops, with scrawny jackrabbits dodging across the road. An occasional carcass of a small dead animal quickly draws the eye's attention as welcome relief from the endless sameness. The flatness has its subtle changes. The black dirt, rich as sin, covers all of Iowa and Nebraska getting a bit more gray as it approaches Illinois. Cutting south from Chicago is Route 66—the highway immortalized by Chuck Berry and the Stones, the funky highway that was driven by George Maharis and Marty Milner in their red Corvette. "Getting your kicks on Route 66" is a mighty challenge in the face of so much bleakness.

When Alabama Wildman heads out of Chicago going home and sees through the windshield the richness of the soil fade from a blackish green to a dusty red, he doesn't need a road map to tell him he's southbound. Names of towns flash by—names like Granite City, Cairo, Funks Grove. This is the southern midwest— where life is as straight as the median line of the Interstate.

Dropping down into Paducah, Kentucky, where the accents soften and the whiskey is bourbon, Alabama Wildman picks up Freddie the Fairy from Tucumcari on the CB radio. Freddie is "jacked up" and broadcasting his original comedy monologue about "the one peter pounder with the two-story outhouse diesel car— eighteen-wheel, fifty-five-foot toilet paper dispenser cleaning out the four wheel sewer…ain't that a bunch of shit. Short stroking this way." But hot on the trail to Skinhead's for some grits, Alabama Wildman doesn't have time to bullshit with Freddie.

Freddie is southbounding down the boulevard talking a mile a minute to nobody special on Channel 10. He's a good old boy whose Freightliner, named "Big Blue," is festooned with Rebel flags and his favorite motto: "When in doubt, whup it out!" As the country starts to take on a slight roll and the homes by the side of the road start to sprout porches, Freddie is in Rebel trucker's heaven. The warm southern air seems to extract the people from inside the houses. They sit and rock and wave as Big Blue rolls by.

Even the signs he passes start to talk in the dialect of the people. A big Black Mammy offers her honey buns only ten miles ahead "fo' yo' breakfast." When he sees "Stop Here, boy, For Catfish," the airbrakes squeal, and Freddie's home.

If a trucker's destination is yet further south, to the Carolinas or Georgia, again the land will spread out before his eyes, and the shifting clay dirt turns a vibrant red-orange. Huge palmetto plants and weary cypress trees, along with overgrown mossy stumps, mix with the slightly acrid air of the Carolina seacoast.

Old southern drivers remember when most all the roads were dirt, and the asphalt was a novelty, but not necessarily a welcome one. Unlike the dirt, it retained the heat it absorbed during the day, and at night cows, drawn by the warmth like an old maid to a hot water bottle, would lie down in the road. The trucks were smaller then, and the impact of a ton of beef on the hoof was akin to that of a brick wall.

From the heaven of the deep south, many a trucker has to make the weekly run through the purgatory of Delaware and the Mid-Atlantic states and into the cold and unfriendly world of New England. What's wrong with it? Ask any trucker, and he'll be happy to tell you about the icy winter and stagnant summer; or about the restaurants that spell grits with a "z," if they serve "gritz" at all; or about northern truckers who don't even have time for a friendly pinball game; or, worst of all, about the roads with potholes big enough to swallow a tire.

Highway 17 up in White River County, Maine, is approximately 300 miles of nothing but dense brush and a moose or two. The roads through the North Woods run past huddled little towns like Jackman and Deer Hollow. But to a driver standing alone beside his broken-down truck, it's the end of the earth. This cold wilderness leaves its stamp on a trucker's memory and has inspired songs like "Tombstone Every Mile" about the Hanesville Woods. Sung by Dick Curless, it is a lament for the "road that has never seen a smile," a road without the security of a pay phone or a house with a lamp in the window.

Kodiak Pete says he was born with ice in his veins, which explains why his favorite stretch of the boulevard is the Alcan Highway. Originating in the Northwest territory of Canada, the Alcan is an awe-inspiring combination of raw beauty and unspeakable danger. Instead of asphalt, the roads are often gravel, miles and miles of small hard pellets flinging themselves against the front of the truck. There are few gas stations and fewer mechanics. Diesel is expensive, and a full tank is necessary at the outset of the trip—so necessary that the Mounties check tank levels before you get on the highway. Kodiak Pete sleeps under furniture pads and fur pelts, and "it takes a mighty good-looking broad to get me out of my thermal underwear."

87

88

Smokey on the prowl

Bold Head Bullfrog would never drive the Alcan because it would take him too far from Piss Hill. Bold Head is a resident of Pennsylvania and he's known about Piss Hill ever since he was a boy. When he started trucking back in the 1930s, his hill was just a brick road where the custom was to stick the truck in Grandma gear, pull out the hand throttle, open the door, stand on the saddle tanks, and piss. "These guys in their king-size cabovers don't know the pleasure of taking a piss on the move."

Whatever its pleasures, Piss Hill isn't enough to make most truckers love "Pennslomania," where the speed limit was fifty-five even before the fuel crisis, and roads like the "Ho-Chi-Minh Trail" (Route 209) try to lose you at every turn.

The Continental Cowboy is less concerned with speed limits than picking the tumbleweed from the radiator of his truck. As he highballs west from Las Cruces to Tucson, the painted desert offers up a bleached palette of shifting sands against a darkening sky. With a load of polyurethane plastics as modern as tomorrow, he re-enters the past when he dismounts his semi and eats at Rose's truck stop, where the taco filling is more armadillo than beef, and the chili is not ersatz, but hot enough to unblock a frozen fuel line.

The more urban towns—Phoenix, Tucson, Albuquerque—have replaced their old ways with cowboy-inspired hamburger stands. The popular joke on the western roads is how you tell a cowboy from a trucker —the answer is the cowboy is wearing sneakers.

The great state of Texas spawns more truckers than anywhere else. Texans, used to spanning great distances to get from place to place, seem to fall naturally into the trucking life. Just as everything in Texas is bigger than anywhere else, a Texan will tell you that the roads are the longest and the widest in the world.

Mr. Ed, a true Texan from the tips of his silver-toed cowboy boots to the broad brim of his ten-gallon hat, is a little more modest than most. But only since his jackknife one night near Falfurrias. Like every other trucker, he used to consider the state trooper a natural enemy, and was always on the lookout for the "County Mountie in a plain blue wrapper." But the night he jackknifed, it was a trooper who helped cut him out of his overturned tractor.

Most truckers believe that the troopers lie in wait for them, eager to search their truck for pills or guns and often treating them with a special, stored-up meanness. When truckers tell you of the elaborate cat and mouse tactics of outwitting smokie, you recall the frantic Tweetie Pie and Sylvester cartoons. Troopers are

often accused of masquerading as truckers on Channel 10 and sending out false messages assuring the truckers they can speed, 'cause there isn't a trooper in sight. And then there's the legendary woman trooper in western Pennsylvania who pulls up beside truckers in an unmarked car, hikes up her skirt, then speeds ahead. Naturally, the trucker follows. As soon as he exceeds 55, she turns on her siren, and one more trucker has fallen into her clever trap.

The Green Weenie doesn't play any such tricks, but he has developed a fearsome reputation among truckers in the midwest. This bear's den is near Pontiac, on Highway 66 in Illinois. When he pulls you over, it better be "yes, officer" or "no, officer," and none of this "okey dokey smokie" routine.

The self-proclaimed kings of the road on eighteen wheels have some respect for the trooper, but little patience for the lowly four-wheelers who take up their space on the highway. A man who has been driving for twenty hours straight can get more than a little pissed off at an absentminded commuter who is hogging the left lane. Something they don't teach in trucking school is the trick of using a little of your forty tons of muscle in a situation like this. Just pull right up to the car with your ten-foot-high cab and give the fellow a nudge and a blast of the air horn. A secret pleasure to many a trucker, tactics like this make the righteous advocates of trucking at American Trucking Association develop ulcers.

As bad as the left-lane hog is the hoo-hooer or the eight-miler. The former is another trucker who sends out unwelcome melodies on his air horn. The latter is a four-wheeler who keeps you guessing his intentions for eight miles or more by leaving on his turn signals.

A bigger challenge than the measly four-wheeler to the trucker "following the bulldog" is the man driving the Greyhound. Although the Greyhound is naturally more fleet-footed than the lumbering bulldog, its human cargo forces it to be more circumspect in its road manners.

Despite the occasional pranks and shows of force, the trucker isn't a bully in a big vehicle, leaving death and destruction in his wake. He is a man trying to make a living driving a truck, and because of the nature of his work, he's involved in more accidents than he'd like to think about. Grisly tales of death and destruction, usually involving friends, seem to be treated more casually by the professional driver. Only when he is alone or thinking about his family do they come back to haunt him.

Fortunately, not all accidents are tragic. The more amusing ones become legends, comforting in their humor. A few years ago two bull haulers collided outside Ogallala, Nebraska, and the scene is said to resemble a Keystone Cops routine, with troopers, truckers, and bulls chasing each other in frantic confusion. The roads were blocked for miles as passing truckers stopped their trucks to help. Thermal-vested matadors, using their bedding as capes and their tire irons as makeshift swords, they stood eye to eye with the bewildered livestock.

The road with all its dangers and conflicts remains the core of a trucker's life. It is the one place he will constantly return to between the women, the cups of coffee, and the holidays spent at home. It's always out there for him, to offer him the escape he dreams of and maybe to trap him at the next curve. It is the stage where all the characters he meets play out their roles, and he remains the star.

Dean

Dean was deadheading south. He was sitting in the yard at the truck lot, halfheartedly polishing the chrome on his Freightliner. The first thing I noticed was the tattoo on his right arm. It was a heart with an arrow through it and the words "Janet my dear" inside. Janet was his ex-wife and when they divorced he had small lines etched into the heart to make it look broken. He said he didn't want to have it taken off altogether out of respect for his children.

Dean asked me into his truck and we spent a few hours shooting the breeze. The tan, creased skin on Dean's face and his pale blue eyes are handsome, marred only by the fact that most of his teeth are missing or have gone bad from neglect.

He looked at me with those pale eyes and said he was feeling bad. He parted his hair and showed me a long scar that traced its way deep into his scalp. Following its contours with his fingers, he recounted the day it happened. Dean had been driving for fifteen hours, and it had been raining since Fargo. He had just gotten off the Interstate to avoid a weigh station, and was weaving his way along a backwoods stretch of road through the brooding hills. He heard nothing and saw no one, but as the sleeves of his shirt started to turn red with his own blood, he felt an icicle of pain cut through his head.

Dean had been shot. Neither the state police nor the local hill people could explain where the bullet came from. The hospital listed it as a "hunting accident," but Dean has known too many other drivers traveling the back roads who have found bullet holes in their trucks miles from anything that's legal hunting.

He recovered well enough to keep driving, but sometimes the pain in his head gets so bad he pulls over to the side of the road, and crawls into the dark sleeper like a wounded animal. Dean said the bullet had never been removed because he refused to stay confined in the hospital long enough for them to operate.

Dean doesn't romanticize his accident or his job. He says he became a truckdriver because he "was too dumb to do much else." After talking to Dean you realize that he's not dumb—just gentle and reticent, and if you're moving too fast these traits get confused.

As I jumped down from the cab of the truck, I turned around to wave good-bye. I could see Dean leaning back against the wall of the sleeper, tenderly rubbing his head.

Nadine

Nadine was nineteen when she died. She was murdered by two truckdrivers from Florida in a motel adjacent to a truck stop in Connecticut. Nadine was a truck-stop whore. She kept her black skin oiled with a fine layer of Vaseline so that she seemed to shine as she passed in front of the trucks' headlights. She wore her hair cut short, almost like a boy's, and would often wear a visored cap turned sideways on her head. She was not good-looking, but she had a high-spirited walk.

Nadine told me she had gotten into prostitution when she ran away from home at sixteen. She hitched up north by truck and when the driver left her off at a truck yard, she just sort of stayed on. Nadine claimed that most of her clients were white southern truckers. I asked her who the northern drivers slept with and she answered, "Each other."

Nadine didn't have a pimp, but she said that the man who runs the motel often took more money from her than he should have. He told her it was for linens and for upkeep, but Nadine knew better. I asked her what she liked about her job and she figured she had it easier than most other hookers because the sleeper cabs were so narrow she didn't have to move around much. Nadine liked to have her picture taken, but she was a night person, and would have nothing to do with standing around in the daylight. Once it got dark, she would strike arrogant poses, hand on hip, and when she heard the shutter snap she would giggle like a child.

She told me she was giving up her profession and going home to Georgia. Just as soon as she could get a ride. She wanted me to bring her some pictures I took of her. She would send these home to her mother with a letter. We arranged to meet at the truck yard in a week. I watched her walk down the long row of trucks, knocking on the doors with her small hand until she finally disappeared into the night.

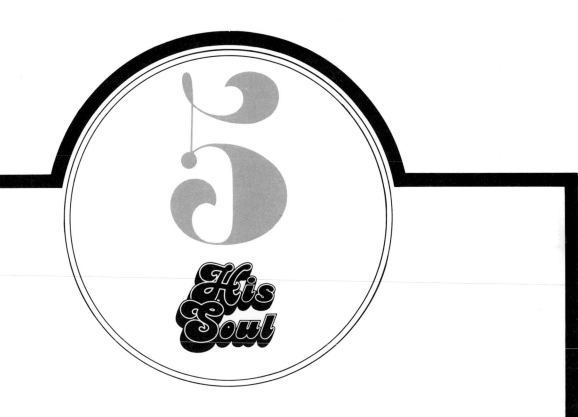

> This world is full of sin, you can see it every day
> Satan is hitchhiking all along the way
> Don't let him ride with you;
> he'll destroy your poor soul.
> Keep your hands on the Bible
> and your eyes on the road.

A trucker's God is a God who drives trucks. His preacher comes to him in a "Chapel on Wheels," and the pews he occupies are inside a semi trailer. The totems of his life fit neatly on the dashboard of his rig. The good luck symbols that will help him over the next icy road or busted bridge hang from his rear-view mirrors, or are glued to the "dogbox." A trucker is likely to refer to Jesus as his "shotgun rider," and his ten commandments can be stretched to include the sins of tampering with a logbook or flirting with a cute waitress while his wife waits at home.

Lighting up the night skies on the Interstates from coast to coast are the fire-and-brimstone chaplains of the "transport for Christ" movement. Emblazoned with illuminated crucifixes, hauling a chapel on wheels, the preachers follow hot on the trail of wayward gear-jammers. Their itinerant flock is gathered from the cooks, waitresses, and laid-over truckers who are in need of salvation. Once they enter the trailer and sit in the narrow pews, they are held spellbound by the evangelistic preaching laced with trucker terminology.

God is the great dispatcher in the sky. The devil may take the form of the big-assed waitress at Smokie's Cafe or the little white pills hidden in the trucker's pocket. When the sermon is finished, Brother Bill hands out copies of "The Highway Evangelist," the Chapel on Wheels Newsletter containing stories of truckers saved from a brush with death and the devil while at the wheels of their semis.

"The Highway Evangelist" keeps you up-to-date on more than sin and salvation. Truckers are alerted to the present danger of their tax money going to savage Indians who like nothing better than feasting on the flesh of young white women, or the government support of the lesbian conspiracy to teach sex education in the schools. Less political articles include the "Silent Wheels" column (obituaries) and "Gearbox Groanings" (accident stories). There are "cute" inserts comparing God to various products, such as VO-5 hairspray, because he holds in all kinds of weather.

But "The Highway Evangelist" doesn't profess to have catalogued the precise details of a trucker's hell. Truckers must depend on legends like "Convoy in the Sky" to provide a vivid picture of the wrong side of forever. The trucker immortalized in this legend is headed down the road with a gnawing guilty conscience when, suddenly cutting across the sky, appears a vision of a fleet of long black semis filled with sinners at their wheels. These drivers' fate is to drive endlessly into the night, never even stopping to coffee up at some celestial truck stop.

Old Bill drove a big green Mack
For a glass works on an East Coast run
He's the best you've ever seen
Took second place to none.

But then one night the Lord saved his soul
Did it right in that big Mack too
Told old Bill to quit the road
He had a bigger job for him to do.

Ol' Bill just shook his head
"Lord, I'm a trucker. That's all I know."
But let me tell you what happened
On his way to Tupelo.

That morning it was cold and starting to snow.
A school bus was stopped down in the road.
He burnt his brakes and stripped his gears
But there was just one place to go.

Bones cracked and metal bent
As asphalt checked his pace
Ol' Bill had run the best he could
But God had won the race.

Men run and sometimes die
To shun the Master's call
'Cause when God can't have the parts he wants
He just up and takes it all.

Could be the trucker carrying the bulky gift-wrapped package under his arm at Christmas time has just bought an original oil painting by Alex Nucklas. When his family opens the package and hangs the picture over the mantle, they will have visible reassurance that safety is indeed in the Lord. Available at the gift shops of almost every large truck stop in the country, these paintings all have similar motifs. Christ is leading a trucker to safety in a storm, pointing the path with one, long elegant finger extending from his gossamer gown. For about ten dollars a trucker can purchase a copy of the painting with "raised brushstrokes," depicting a blond or brunet Christ looking a little like the hitch-hiking hippy the trucker passed on the road. He appears from a cloud of diesel smoke or a storm cloud and rescues the trucker in the nick of time from a deadly collision or fall off the mountainside.

Many believe that, for all his swagger, the trucker is a lost lamb afloat in a sea of sin, desperately searching for a safe port. "Preacher Man," the CB handle for the Reverend Jimmy Snow, has spent the past ten years working to reach these drivers. He is perhaps the most famous of those looking after the trucker's soul, as he is not only the son of country-western Hall of Famer Hank Snow, but also a star of his own weekly show from the stage of the Grand Ol' Opry. Among the multitude of gearjammers who flock to his sermons you'll find Johnny Cash, Connie Smith, and other Nashville aristocrats.

Jimmy Snow first started using the CB radio when he realized that truckers were not staying around Nashville long enough to attend his sermons. He admits that many of them tune out when they realize that the "Preacher Man" they are talking to is a real preacher, but he has two cardboard boxes filled with testimonials from truckers who have been saved. His wife, herself a country-western singer coiffed in the Dolly Parton style of mountainous blond curls, helps stir the spirit of his congregation as he preaches.

Reverend Jimmy Snow
Nashville, Tennessee

99

Just Me, This Old Truck, and My Lord

You know that old highway can sure get lonesome
Long about three in the mornin'
That late at night things get kinda quiet
And you wish you were home with your wife and young'uns
But I always got a passenger with me
And he keeps me from getting bored
If you were out there, you could hear me say
There's just me, this old truck, and my Lord
Yeah, he's made a lot of miles with me
Up and down that long white line
In fact we've got better than a million
    safe driving miles
But the credit sure ain't all mine
Why I wouldn't think of startin' on a run
Without asking him to climb aboard
'Cause when I'm out there and it's late at night
There's just me, that old truck, and my Lord
Now he always rides on the right hand side
Sorta leaves the driving up to me
But I've called on him a lotta times
When it was storming, snowing, getting hard to see
And many is the night
We've been on ice
That rig started spinning like Maria
And I'd just kinda glance across the cab and say
"Lord, how 'bout you takin' the wheel"
And that's exactly what he'd do
'Cause we always managed to get back home
And then I'd never forget to say "Thank you Lord
It was sure nice having you along"
Yeah, he's always been right there when I needed him
Whether it be noon or three A.M.
So I think it's high time that I make a promise
That I'm gonna be better to him
For you see my time can't be much longer
Riding up and down that road
And I just hope when it comes
And I make that final run
You can still hear me say
There's just me, this old truck, and my Lord.

Joe West

One tragedy of the trucking life that even religion can't change is the day that a truckdriver must pull off the road forever. Truckdriving burns a man out quick. It is rare that a man over fifty-five can be found still driving the long-haul rigs. The day-to-day uncertainty and the constant movement starts to eat away at the soul. It isn't a gold watch that marks the end of a truck-driver's life. It is the feeling that he would rather stay home.

Every trucker knows that the time will come that he will sit on the porch and watch the others roll by on the highway, and he secretly dreads facing the future with the few friends and diminished family that the trucking life leaves you.

There was a wreck down Harlan way
Just before the dawn
Big Joe from Louisville
Laid his Ol' Mack down.

Big Joe had made that run
Since his truckin' life began
That Mack was brand new his first day out
And they started hand in hand.
Thirty years without an accident
Makes you wonder what went wrong.

Well Big Joe was up for retirement
And do you think it just might be
The man couldn't bear to leave his truck
Or his truck say goodbye to he?

Sometimes his truck does seem like a driver's only friend. While he might carry a St. Christopher's medal and a rabbit's foot in his pocket, a trucker will further insure his truck's safety with the purchase of lucky chattering skulls and perhaps even a sprinkling of holy water at one of the roadside chapels incorporated into some of the large truck stops. The windows of these chapels are decaled with stained-glass Contac paper and their walls are the same peach pink cinderblock as those in the bunkhouse, but the tacky surroundings don't keep the gearjammers away.

After weeks without seeing the same face twice or stopping to see how far he's traveled, he looks forward to the day he finally pulls into his own driveway—even though his kids might not know him, and his wife doesn't look the same. He is amazed at how this island

of sanity stays together without him. In his mind's eye the children's growth stopped when he left, and his wife, apple pie in hand, slowed to a halt, to be re-awakened only at his next homecoming.

Mama waved goodbye from the kitchen
As I smelled an apple pie cooking loud
The kids were outside playing baseball
They just smiled between a home run and an out.

They're just simple 'bout my leaving
They're just simple 'bout my being gone
If I didn't really know them better
I'd swear they don't miss me at all.

If his truck is fast enough and he is strong enough, he will be able to outrun the devil and the woman looking to tie him down with piles of bills and kids needing braces. There may be other answers for life's problems —psychiatry, meditation, or even dying—but he has found the answer that works best for him: traveling.

There ain't nothing this side of heaven
Can chase away my ills
Like two chrome stacks blowing black
Over eighteen singing wheels.

The passion that brings a man to spend his life driving millions of miles can sometimes inspire a singular kind of poetic expression. What many see as a lumbering vehicle of steel and rubber can be transformed in the trucker-poet's eyes into a vision of erotic beauty:

I met a beautiful lady
All dressed in a silver coat
She said she felt like wandering
And would I like to go.

We climbed the highest mountain
And crossed the rolling sea
And rolled into adventure
Just this silver lady and me...

102

Whether cradled as a child on the metal breast of a diesel truck, or taken to his grave by one, a trucker who is moved to reflect upon his own life finds his inspiration in the tedious routine that makes up most of truckdriving. Country-western songs about truck-driving dwell on the adventures encountered rolling down the highway. But only a real trucker knows the agony of driving so long and so far that your leg cramps up so bad you can't walk down the steps of your truck. Trucking is endless driving—and waiting. Between the long hauls, especially for the independent driver, come the sometimes even longer waits. Ask Charlie up at the Mass 10 Truck Stop who pulled in from California four months ago and has been looking for a load that will pay his way back ever since.

Sunday is always the worst day at the truck stop. It's a handful of lonely owner-operators with nowhere to go and nothing to haul. Maybe Monday will bring that phone call and the load they've been waiting for. Meanwhile, they're trying to make a weekend.

Guess I'll have another cup of coffee
Might as well, help pass the time
Wish I had a run going somewhere
Maybe rolling would ease my troubled mind.

Jukebox ain't stopped since seven
But then the music ain't too bad
Kinda soothes the pain and makes it better
When a fella's down and feeling bad.

Little blonde there behind the counter
Said she'd join me if I had a mind
But I'll just sit this one out solitary
After all, I'm just killing time.

Nothing's wrong that won't be right
When Monday rolls around
It's just that I'm trying to make a weekend
With my baby out of town.

A trucker with a poetic eye sees in even the most mundane encounters a vision of the romance of the road.

I was over in Waycross, Georgia
Tryin' to get a little fuel
When in pulled this big Freightliner
And told the jockey to fill her full.

He climbed down off that country Cadillac
And walked around to me
He had on a pair of the prettiest boots
I reckon I ever did see.

He reached for his cigarette pack
And shook him out one or two
And said "I just got to take me one
"Ol' Buddy how 'bout you?"

And I said "Pillheads and Cowboys and Truck-drivin' men"
They're all out there tonight riding that silver wind
So if you're headin' down the highway
Be careful there, my friend
Of those Pillheads and Cowboys and Truckdrivin' men.

If you have diesel smoke in your veins and white-line fever inflames your soul then you're a truckdriver and you want to express those feelings. It might seem incongruous to think of a big and burly truckdriver taking pen in hand and translating his feelings into verse, but like his cowboy, sailor, and traindriving ancestors it is sometimes the most fulfilling way to cope with the brutality of the road. A man can't live with the constants of accidents, death, loneliness, and lack of family ties without some kind of outlet. Some look no further than the pinball machine or the CB radio, but others create songs, prayers, and drawings, all revolving around a central theme—trucks.

It is rare for any profession in the 1970s to produce such self-serving art. When was the last time you ran into an accountant who writes poems to computers, or a dentist who knows at least ten songs about pyorrhea. But then it is equally unusual to find a dentist, accountant, or anyone else who spends as much time living his profession as a trucker.

104

Reverend Snow's evangelical fleet

The Chapel on Wheels

The poems are not sophisticated or polished. They roll like a loaded semi straight to the heart where the impact of their simple sentiments make a deep impression. With his hands gripping the steering wheel the trucker-poet hears the rhythm of his tires set the meter for his next poem—a poem written for himself, and anyone else who knows about a road-loving soul.

There's a lot of rough old roads you'll have to travel
And there's a lot of days you'll have rough old times
But once you've set behind that big ol' throttle
Nothing else can ever ease your mind

Oh, if I could answer that call.
To that diesel lure I'd say
I'd set sail on her concrete sea
And sail my life away.

6

His Truckstop

It's been a long night on the Interstate, and the uniformed and well-regulated crew of the shiny chrome truck stop doesn't know it, but Pete has passed out in a puddle of grease by the main entrance. It isn't serious—too many pills and too little sleep. Not twenty feet from coffee, but he couldn't make it. A Greyhound unloads a cluster of Japanese tourists. Some of the women head for the long row of shining white ten-cent-a-shot E-VAC-U-WAIT toilets. Others stand in line for their microwave road-burgers. One of the group approaches the prostrate driver and snaps a quick series of shots with his Nikon. The flash does nothing to wake Pete. The Japanese rejoins his group by politely stepping over him. Hobos hoping for a free meal loiter nearby, not far from the RecVee's and campers of suburban families on vacation.

Pete hasn't been driving for long. He learned his trade at a school for truckers, where he graduated sixth in his class. He was assigned as a co-driver on an old trucker's rig. His first day out he admitted he didn't know the first thing about driving a truck. He told his co-driver, who listened sympathetically, that for $500 he had learned to go in a straight line. The old trucker showed him how to drive, but within a month Pete will retire from truckdriving and take an office job. Lying face down on a bed of concrete isn't the glory of the open road he had anticipated.

Ten miles down the road is another truck stop known only to the veteran drivers who have been around since before the construction of the Interstate. It is almost 2:00 A.M. as Brigham Passer pulls onto the concrete apron of the Red Ace. Everything else on Route 100 is closed as tight as a clam's ass, but it's rush hour at the Red Ace. Inside Margo barely has time to adjust her blond wig which has the habit of slipping down over her forehead when she wrinkles her brow. Her waitress uniform is tradition itself. The white dress is a nylon material that brings to mind bleached celery. A pale blue cardigan is held together over her breast by a gold chain with a poodle on either end whose jaws grip the edges of the blue wool. Her stockings have a run, and the shoes she wears have had a scissors taken to them to give her toes a little more room.

Margo spots Brigham's truck through the window as he applies the air brakes. Brigham has always been pretty special to her. He has been coffeeing up here for more than eight years, and in the fifteen years Margo's been waitressing, she's never met a trucker she's liked as much.

She asks Helen, the other waitress, to take over for her, grabs her purse from under the counter and heads for the bathroom. She sits on the lid of the toilet seat and locks the stall door. The smell of room deodorizer is overpowering—a full-bodied rose scent mixed with the smell of the old fixtures. From her bag Margo extracts a thick roll of bills, mainly fives and tens, but big enough to make the red rubber band around them strain. She snaps away the elastic band and starts to count. There is more than $300, a good part of which will be her share from the sale of Brigham's bennies. He likes to drop down to Nogales or Mexicali on the weekend and buy the bennies at a drugstore where they are legal. His price is a penny apiece, and he sells them easily for ten cents a shot back in the states. His greasy-spoon sales force usually keep fifty percent for their troubles.

Brigham has been on the road for twenty-eight years and considers himself a model driver—no reported accidents, no speeding tickets, and no time in jail— except for the usual kangaroo court on a side road where he was picked up trying to avoid a weigh station. He considers his dope-selling an aid to other truckers who have to stay awake to pull in the green stamps.

Margo slips the wadded bills into her apron pocket, proud she has sold so many pills, and glad she has some extra cash. She adjusts the wig again, plumping it up with the end of her rat-tailed comb, and gives herself a long spray from the White Shoulders atomizer in her purse....

The Red Ace used to be a more profitable place to work. About fifteen years ago, it was considered a large truck stop. Located on what was the main road before the Interstate was built, it was the only diesel island for two hundred miles in any direction. It had showers for the drivers, and a bunk house for fifty cents a night. Now the bunks are all boarded up, and the showers are the domain of the palmetto bugs that love the dank darkness of the mildewed stalls. The only things still standing with conviction are the pumps and the little cafe. The Red Ace sign is unhinged and swinging in the soft wind.

Inside are two pinball machines and a juke box and a blackboard where the menu of the day is written in chalk: "Meat 2 Veg." A Red Ace regular would never think of asking what kind of meat. It's the truck-stop standard, an ominously dark thing—probably a pot roast that has been simmering a good fifteen hours or so, the fibers broken apart and the cartilage surrendered to the assault of handfuls of tenderizer. The meat has taken on the tired look of the men who eat it. The veg is an anemic platter of string beans, and with it comes an ice cream scoop full of mashed potatoes. At the Red Ace, quantity is the substitute for quality.

There are about twelve other drivers in the booths along the wall. Brigham spots Cajun Joe and Crawdaddy, two CB-loving truckdrivers from Louisiana. Between them sits Jolene, "The Bayou Queen." She has a CB radio in her whorehouse in New Orleans, and she contacts truckers on the road to guide them to her house of pleasure. Jolene is dressed in hot pants and knee-high white stretch boots. Her hair is a mountain of immobile, frosted curls. Before she became a hooker, Jolene worked as a waitress at the Red Ace.

She can remember when the Red Ace, like many other truck stops, was more of a road hazard than a friendly oasis. Twenty or thirty years ago, truckdrivers and travelers were ripped off as frequently as they were serviced. Two pots of coffee were kept brewing on the stove, one pot for regulars and lucky strangers who aroused no interest, and the other, laced with knock-out drops, for an easy mark with a full money belt. Many old-timers never took a drop of coffee from an unknown diner. The danger of the roadside cafe followed the driver into the bunk house. Before sleeper cabs were introduced, a trucker slept in either his driver's seat or the trailer of his truck and a room with a bed was tempting, even if it had to be shared with strangers. A trucker who was a light sleeper, or who couldn't fall asleep to a lullaby of assorted snores, was

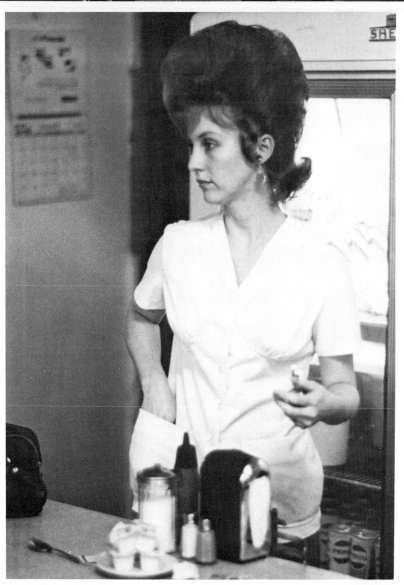

112

The Red Ace Truck Stop
South Carolina

in for a long night. Many a fight occurred between a man who had drunk himself into a loud, snoring sleep and a bunkmate, pilled-up and feisty about the noise. A trucker protected his wallet well, since he often had to carry large sums of money.

Today if a trucker wants to escape the narrow confines of his truck, he can rent a motel room at a truck stop for around ten dollars a night. The rooms aren't lavishly decorated like the ones at a Holiday Inn, but the cinder-block walls are painted a frothy seafoam green, and the hypnotic eye of TV tube has a soothing quality that can iron out the tensions of the road. The driver can be paged in his room at any time by the built-in loud speaker, telling him to move his truck or to wake up and hit the road. Somewhere in every truck stop is a row of pay phones. Even in the middle of the night, they will be occupied by wildcatters looking for loads or lonely men calling their wives.

As the morning light rises on Columbia City or Phoenix or Roanoke, drivers rinse the old coffee taste from their mouths, and get ready to enjoy one of the delights of life on the road, the best meal a truck stop can offer— breakfast. Southern breakfasts in particular are special. The grits and biscuits with milk or red-eye gravy complement the country ham or pork chops. Even the dingiest truck stop can usually produce biscuits that are lighter than air and a slab of cured ham that shames the rubbery pink substitute that is served up north.

The menu at a truck stop bears witness to the size of the drivers' appetites. Eight eggs and toast is not an unusual item on a breakfast menu. For dinner you can order a "tanker of stew." The price of such meals reflects their size, and then some. A trucker hopes to get his money's worth. He knows, though, that a skinny hamburger isn't a bargain even if it's called a "tandem special," and a plate of watery pasta tastes bad even when the menu bills it as "a truckload of spaghetti."

"Once that cup hits the counter, it's gotta be kept filled" were the boss's first words to Judy, now a veteran truck-stop waitress of twelve years. Whether it's called "hundred-mile coffee," "java," "road tar," or "bennie chaser" it's the life blood coursing through the veins of the highway drivers. The trucker needs caffeine fuel like his truck needs diesel. Black, blacker, blackest, and hot as hell, hundreds of thousands of gallons are poured down road-parched throats.

If you eliminate all the big truck plazas and their microwave oven disasters that give truckers the ulcers they are prone to, then eliminate the little greasy spoons like the Red Ace, owned by men whose main concern

is selling a little fuel and whose kitchen hobbles along on some old prison cook's creations, you will be left with the "Ma-and-Pa" truck stops. They are small family-run fuel stations that are an easy pleasure to imagine and a tricky challenge to find. Juicy steaks, stews, and home-baked pies are plentiful and cheap. Like the food, the decor is usually homemade. Ma-and-Pa truck stops have a corner on the jokes, gags, and souvenir market. Joy buzzers, whoopie cushions, funny slogans, and salt and pepper shakers with the states' names on them abound. If you are lucky, Florence, the owner of the Home Cooken Cafe in Oregon, will pull her rubber-chicken joke on you. If you order the roast chicken dinner that she suggests, you will be served the rubber substitute nestled in a bed of potatoes. The hilarity of the rubber chicken hasn't diminished in ten years, and will probably be around for another ten. Despite the gags, truck stops like Florence's were the start of the rumors that travelers should eat where they see trucks parked, since truckers "know all the good places."

Locations of good truck stops were passed on through word of mouth. The most talked about, however, are not necessarily the best. The Mass 10 Truck Stop, one of the most publicized in the country, is really a variation of the Emperor's New Clothes. Referred to even by its owner as "The Dump," Mass 10 is almost hidden by a gargantuan billboard sign advertising itself. It is a very small yellow stucco building the size of a small-town gas station. But in addition to the diner across the street and a drivers' lounge that looks like a nostalgiac's dream of the 1950s, Mass 10 has a lot to offer the road-weary.

Gene Murphy and his two Great Danes reign over this small truck-stop empire known to drivers coast to coast. What makes Mass 10 unique is that Murphy is a benevolent ruler who shares his kingdom with the men of the road. They get free bunks for the night, free showers, and free access to his summer lake house. And if they're broke, he'll probably give them a loan. He's gotten everything from sides of beef to a gross of frozen TV dinners in return, but Gene Murphy gets the biggest kick out of the more than fifty kids who have been named after him by their truckdriver fathers.

The men at Mass 10 congregate in the drivers' lounge where the television set is always on. The large, glaring image is the only light in a room kept darkened for the benefit of tired eyes.

But soothing isn't always what a trucker's after. For an alternative, he may go to Naked City, the country's only nude truck stop. He will be greeted at the door by

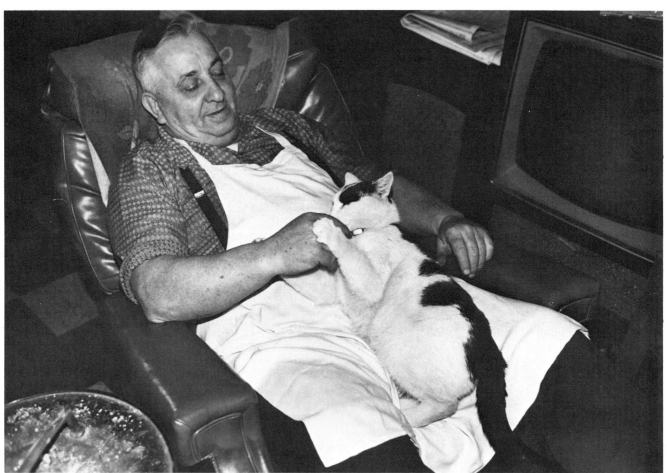

The cook and his cat, Karen's Truck Stop
Billings, Montana

Truck-stop interior
Hope, Arkansas

Cover Girl Cheryle, the hostess and also reigning Miss Nude America. It is Cheryle's job to keep the truckers happy, and she doesn't mind if a stray hand occasionally wanders towards one of her silicone breasts. At Naked City, the waitresses, truckers, cooks, and helpers are all nude. Because of its location near a nudist colony, there is little problem getting undressed help. Even the chef at the restaurant is nude, except for his chef's cap and long white apron. His bare buttocks are no doubt the inspiration for his handle "Southern Exposure."

Many truckers are skeptical upon hearing about Naked City. The notion of a nude truck stop plunked down in Roselawn, Indiana, in the heart of Ku Klux Klan country seems far fetched—like another tall tale unleashed by a bored driver. Even when one pulls down the long driveway towards the mirrored building that is Naked City, the reality isn't much more believable.

Owner Dick Drost, confined to a wheelchair because of muscular dystrophy, talks to truckers on the road using his CB handle, "Nude Wheels." An entrepreneur, his enterprises fan out from the Naked City truck complex to include such diverse schemes as renting jets to the FBI and holding the annual "Mister Nude Trucker" contest.

116

Behind the one-way mirror walls, for three dollars a day, truckers can indulge in sauna baths and whirlpool tubs, admire the limousines on display—once owned by Dean Rusk and Jerry Lewis but now carpeted in pink mohair—and, best of all, parade around nude, except for their hats and cowboy boots, while chatting with nude hostesses.

At night while the semis idle on the parking strip that occasionally serves as an airplane runway, the truckers enter the diner with an elegant facade and an interior as funky as any midwest truck stop can be. Over huge slabs of ham and fries, with only Cokes to wet their palates, they are treated to a Reddi-Wip-and-honey dessert, with Miss Nude America serving as the human plate. Whether it is the strain of hours on the road, or just the bizarre, unreal quality of life at a nude truck stop, there is a strange lack of sexual tension in the air.

Cheryle often sits watching one of the dozen TV sets at Naked City, perched on the small towel that keeps her famous behind from sticking to the Lucite chair, while truckers, also nude or dressed as their tastes prefer, drift off to play with the pet raccoon or read the newspaper.

There is much laughing and groaning during Cheryle's nightly performance, but after she's given every trucker

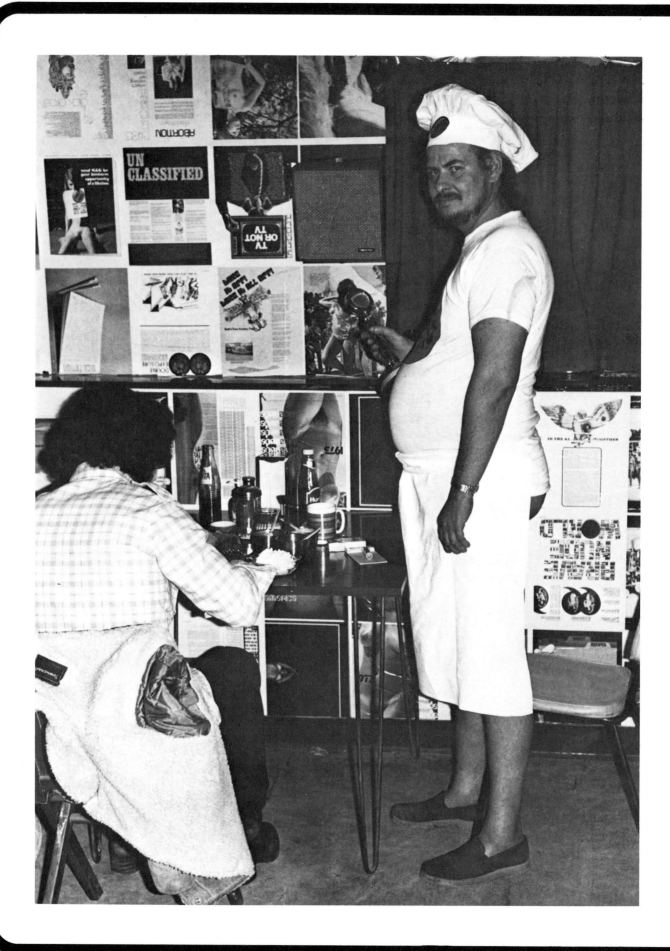

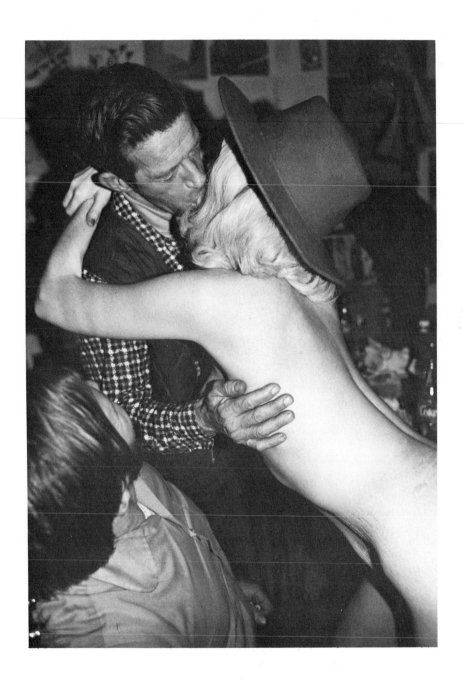

119

"Southern Exposure," the cook
 (left)

Miss Nude America makes friends with a
trucker

121

a goodnight kiss and a souvenir balloon, they wash the honey off their hands, climb back into their trucks, and hit the road. The tone of life at Naked City is like any other truck stop in the country, only with more goose bumps.

Most truck stops are not endowed with the fleshy facilities of Naked City, but there are very few that lack a pinball machine. Pinball is the major, big-league truck-stop sport. Many a man has come home empty handed after losing a paycheck in nickles and dimes betting on the pinball machines. At 4:00 A.M. you can hear the sound of the little silver balls crashing against the sides of the machines as men huddle over them in deep concentration. With the concern he shows when beating the truck's tires to check for a slow leak, the pinball expert will even up the table by precisely tapping the legs. Pinball is a ritual. There are men who think that dimes minted after 1950 are unlucky. Some put the dime in heads up. Others will tap it on the heel of their boot before they play. The proper stance is to grab the machine by the sides, not rocking it, but somehow sweet-talking it with body language.

If you've lost your shirt at pinball, but still have a few dollars left, you can always buy a new one in the ever present truck-stop gift store. Merchandise here ranges from the useful to the ridiculous. Paintings on velvet depict Jesus leading a truck to safety in a storm. There are plastic seat cushions and laminated plaques titled, "What Is a Trucker's Wife," an endless list of heartaches which a woman at home must endure. Inflatable Mack bulldogs, bulldog ashtrays, as well as keychains, watch fobs, and belt buckles adorned with the scowling sourmug fill the cases. A trucker's belt buckle is a small advertisement for himself. The classic buckle is a truck enameled in red or blue with the driver's name on it. The roster includes bizarre handles such as "Phalix," "Roscoe," "Butch," "Doc," "Hooks," "Reuvan," "Goober," and some that sound like a roll call for the seven dwarfs.

For wives and lovers, the trucker can select from a large assortment of charm bracelets and earrings. The motif is often a winged rubber tire rimmed with the word "sweetheart."

In addition to the jewelry, most truck stops sell the basic clothing needed for the road. A man can find cowboy boots, thermal vests, "two-speed gloves," and "gearshift caps," in addition to shirts and pants. The prices are very high, but since drivers aren't likely to pull their rigs up to Bloomingdale's to do comparison shopping, they are a captive market. One hot item they sell that Bloomingdale's doesn't carry is party tapes.

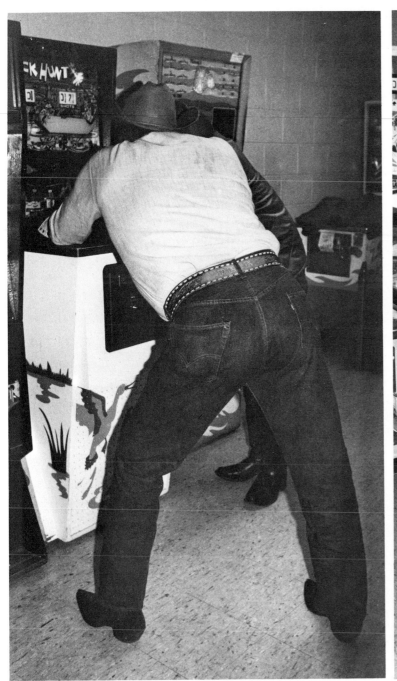
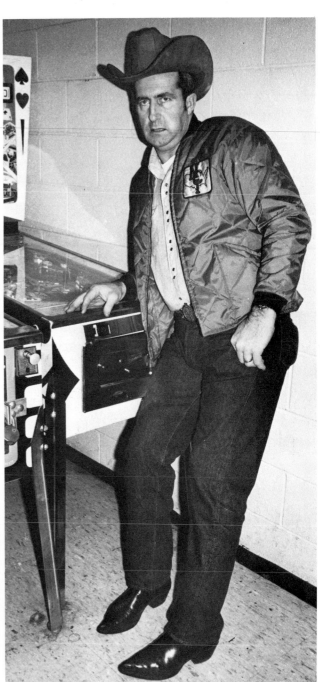

126

"Hundred-mile" coffee

With titles like "Pull My Gearshift" or "Chrome Knockers," they complement the country-western music that is the trucker's favorite.

After a man has outfitted himself, he can do the same for his truck. Custom truck accessories include such goodies as silver bulldogs with red light-up eyes, long-necked swans, winged women, electric religious icons, leatherette toss pillows and lamb's wool seat-covers. When a trucker isn't dressing up his truck, he may be building a scale model of it. Or he can buy stickers and decals to put on his truck advertising his political, sexual, or CB radio affiliation. Between *Penthouse* and *Playboy* are the trucker magazines, *Overdrive, Owner-Operator,* and *Open Road. Overdrive,* the most controversial because of its activist stance, places "the price of truth" at $2.50, another stab in the chain-drive pocketbook. You'll find No-Doz in most truck-stop stores, but not many buyers. For the real stay-awake medicine, truckers look elsewhere...

At the Red Ace, Margo feels her wig start to slip again. One hand goes to her hairline, while the other goes down to smooth out the bulge the money is making in her flimsy apron. Margo knows that Brigham is a hamburger man, and for those who want more than Meat 2 Veg, the grill is always open. She slaps on a few patties as Brigham walks through the door. The air is heavy with the smell of fuel and sweat. Sam, who runs the Red Ace, is pushing a mop around the floor. From a large table, a driver approaches Margo, asking if she has anything that would pass as a birthday cake. It's for Jimmy, a retired trucker whose birthday is today. Margo finds an old brownie baked earlier in the week and a sparkler from the Fourth of July which she puts in the middle.

It is three o'clock, time for the nightly police visit. This is the smokies' time to hang up the new wanted posters on the bulletin board. A new hijack poster usually warrants some attention. The board is always covered with notes left by truckers. "Little Joe wants Sweetmeat to meet him in Frisco." "Contact Wyoming Bighorn if you know of any loads to Dago."

Whenever the troopers come in, Margo gets nervous. With her secret stash of black mollies and white crosses hidden in the towel dispenser of the ladies' room and the $300 in her apron, she is aware of her hand shaking as she pours a cup of coffee for the trooper. Sadusky, the trooper, is showing Sam a package of porno pictures he took from a "homo" he arrested at a rest stop. Sam asks if he can have a few for his collection, and Margo pretends not to hear.

Sadusky finally picks up his broad-rimmed hat and lifts his broad-beamed rear off the counter stool. Brigham gets up from the table where he's been sitting, and walks over to Margo, who is filling the cream pitchers on the counter. The pitchers are in the shape of cow heads, and the milk pours out through the mouth, like vomit. Sam thought they were "cute" and ordered fifty, with "Red Ace" printed on them, from the salesman.

Brigham motions her outside to his waiting truck. She asks Helen to take over again and under Sam's annoyed glance, walks outside into the cool 4:00 A.M. air. She climbs up the metal steps of Brigham's Freightliner, swings herself into the seat and for the first time that evening, Brigham meets her glance. He smiles and leans back in the driver's seat, and Margo is aware of how quiet it is compared to the inside of the cafe. She notices the disarray of his bunk, the slightly soiled sheets and extra blankets pushed into a heap. A sweaty male odor permeates the cab and mixes with the smell of cigarette butts in the ashtray.

Brigham punches up a stereo cassette and Del Reeves voice robs the truck of its silence as she gives him the roll of bills. He leans over and kisses her awkwardly over the dogbox. He asks her when she'll get off work, and if she will meet him at the motel down the road. She agrees and she reaches under the mattress and pulls out a large bottle of West Coast turnarounds. He asks her if she could sell them as fast as the others and in a quiet voice, Margo tells Brigham that she doesn't like selling the pills. She's too nervous with the stash in the ladies' room, but maybe next month when the bills pile up again.

Brigham jumps out of the truck and walks around to her side to help her out. Margo isn't very good at negotiating the steps going down the side of the cab, and often tears her stockings. Brigham calls out the name of the motel to her as she walks towards the Red Ace. As she hears the truck's air brakes release, she starts to hum the Del Reeves song. Brigham pulls the rig out on the road and heads for the motel. He isn't at all worried about getting the pills sold. He knows Mary Louise in Portland will be glad to do it, or that new cute one in San Jose. He isn't worried at all.

The Red Ace and truck stops like it have seen others like Margo and Brigham come and go. From night shift to day, and from one truck stop to another, the same dramas will be played out with the same characters—the road-weary drivers looking for home-style

129

The truckers' lounge
Mass 10 Truck Stop

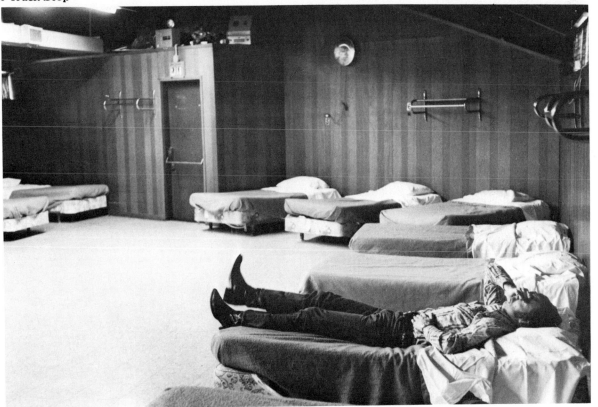

The bunkhouse

comforts and companionship, and the waitresses numbed by the endless passage of faces over an infinite sea of coffee.

But it's more than coffee and fuel that make a truck stop. Ask Gene Murphy or others like him who have spent years filling the needs of those lonely men whose few stationary hours demand that the truck stop offer a roadside facsimile of home. He'll tell you with knowing sympathy that these "modern bedouins," who prefer a tent over their truck rather than a shelter for themselves, need the open arms of home without the grasping hands. Once inside the "truckers only" swinging doors of even the most modern auto-truck complex,

there is a world as comforting to a trucker as the easy chair at home is to an ordinary man.

On the surface, truck stops don't seem to change much from place to place. Of course, some are fancier than others, and the juke boxes are usually regional. You'll rarely find the Rolling Stones and Hank Williams as disc-mates in the same box. The big truck stops hire better-looking waitresses; oftentimes college girls on summer vacation getting their first taste of road life from behind a coffee pot. Then there are the stops that you would drive right past if you didn't know better. They are hardly identifiable as truck stops, except for an asphalt yard out front big enough to hold a rig or two.

Weenieville

132

Beneath a giant painting of a hot dog, you'll find the "all new" Weenieville truck stop. It's a low white building set way back on an old road in Durham, Connecticut, and despite the sign, the regulars know that nothing's changed in fifteen years. New or old, Weenieville is an anachronism in this age of the huge truck complex. It doesn't offer its patrons overnight facilities, nor does it have a drivers' lounge, wall-to-wall Naugahyde, or a color TV. Weenieville has no telex, no magazine stand, not even a fuel pump. What it does have is Nancy.

Nancy is the waitress. *The* waitress, as opposed to *a* waitress, because Weenieville is a two-person operation; a cook and a waitress. Nancy is twenty now and has been at Weenieville for three years. She wouldn't win any beauty contests, and she'll be the first to tell you. She is circus fat, and glistens with a layer of cooking grease, but her round, swarthy face has a definite charm and after a while it becomes apparent why the trucks pull in time after time under the sign of the giant wiener.

Nancy loves truckdrivers, but not in the casual manner of a college girl looking for stories to carry back to the dorms in September. The day I first met Nancy it was at least ninety-eight humid degrees out. She was behind the counter, one hand on her hip, juggling a neat stack of wheatcakes over a griddle for some old gear-

jammer. The place was filled with flies, and an old radio was the only entertainment, but nobody seemed to care because there was Nancy. Nancy is Pearl Mesta, Dick Cavett, and Gertrude Stein; the four greasy walls of Weenieville and the half-dozen regulars perched on their row of stools comprise her salon.

Weenieville is unique but not alone. On the back roads of the American highways are hundreds of tiny oases like it. Some, like "that little place down around Plano, Texas," don't have names but they are all the breeding grounds for the legends of truckdriving. Nancy's special fire is a spark and a connection. She's as much a part of trucking as the long roads that connect truck stop to truck stop. She knows more about the men of the road than most of their wives do, and even though she'd never trade her coffee pot for a gearshift, a little piece of her soul is always on the road.

There is something magic happening in broken-down Weenieville that is destroyed under the neon lights of the big truck complexes. As Nancy dishes out chipped beef on toast or calls out for an order of "cackles on a raft," she is center stage. A fresh refill of coffee appears as soon as a cup is half-empty. Deftly moderating a half-dozen conversations, Nancy encourages the re-telling of tales she has heard countless times before.

136

138

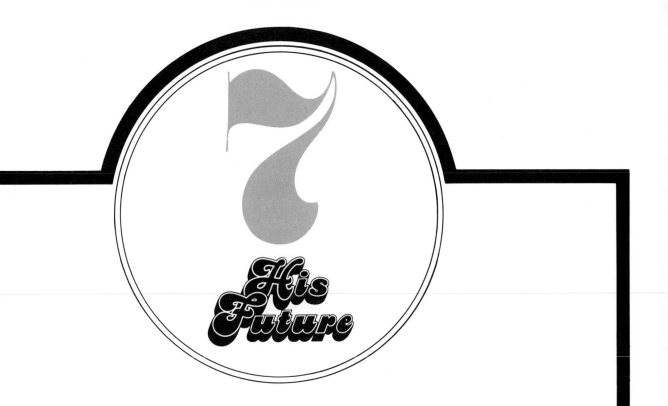

7

His Future

It was as swift and potentially lethal as the sting of a scorpion. On the morning of January 31, 1974, the nation was first stunned then paralyzed by the actions of a group of people traditionally known for their political indifference. The nation's truckers had always been invisible in an age of militant protest. Their role in providing the goods needed to keep the country moving was so efficient as to be taken for granted. Like a dependable, well-oiled machine, trucking efficiency went unnoticed until it broke down.

The first nationwide truck shutdown, scripted by *Overdrive* Magazine and inspired by President Nixon's fuel hikes, was a drama played out on the nation's highways and Interstates. Suddenly men who called themselves improbable names like Coyote or Dangerous Dan were holding America's fate in the same hands that were usually wrapped around a steering wheel. The nation sat at home, eyes focused on their TV screens, listening to the demands for price rollbacks and speed limit hikes. The chips were, as usual, stacked in the government's favor, and although 21 million strong, the trucker rebellion proved a toothless tiger.

The lifeline of this country is the road that the trucker travels, and its blood is the produce he hauls. When the truckers stopped driving, supermarket shelves and drugstore racks depleted. For a few weeks the trucker

Somewhere South of Nashville

Someone called from somewhere south of Nashville
Said they saw a big old diesel by the highway laying down
Someone called from somewhere south of Nashville
Wanted to know if you were Nashville bound.

I said you left somewhere in the midnight of my memory
Can't remember which way you were bound
But I heard you turning north round Franklin Crossing
When you geared that big old Jimmy down.

Then someone called from somewhere south of Nashville
Said they saw a big old diesel by the highway laying down
Someone called from somewhere south of Nashville
Wanted to know if you were Nashville bound.

I just could not remember which way you said you were going
Though I know you must have said a hundred times
But in the cold cold rain where you lay dying
You knew exactly where I was all the time.

Then someone called from somewhere south of Nashville
Said they saw a big old diesel by the highway laying down
Someone called from somewhere south of Nashville
And I knew at that moment you were Nashville bound
Yes, I knew at that moment you were Nashville bound.

Jack Hamilton
Truckdriver

was a national hero. Ballsy and tough as his legend, it seemed he could do what the rest of the country couldn't. He could give the ruling powers tit for tat — no fuel…no goods. And there he was, catapulted in his thermal vest and driving gloves, into the halls of Congress.

The shutdown was dramatic, and supplied a wealth of new stories and myths to exchange at the truck stops. It gave the modern trucker the opportunity to flex his muscles, to surface through the myth of his slightly archaic existence, to show his face and speak his piece. It gave the public a chance to see the men and women who bring them their every necessity. What it did not do was to roll back prices or change the speed limit; and some say it just made the trucker-trooper issue worse.

If you listen to the truck magazines or the teamsters you get the impression that the truckers were eagerly awaiting a leader to harness all that power and muscle into one grand voice. This notion was the fatal flaw of the shutdown. The thing a trucker holds most dear, the very thing that put him on the road in the first place, is his lust for independence. Nobody, not even another trucker, tells him what to do. He functions on his own judgments and he comes and goes as he pleases, bristling at the mountains of paperwork he must complete on each run, and scrupulously avoiding anything that will impede his freedom.

Bob Richardson from Vermont will tell you what happened to him on January 31. "You know, it's funny about the shutdown. I was all for it. I was hardly breaking even with the price of fuel. As an owner-operator, I have a big loan out on my rig, and I have to work heavy hours to get enough to pay my bills and all. Anyway, I was in Youngstown the night before. I pulled into the truck stop around 3:00 A.M. and just climbed into my bunk and went to sleep. In the morning I was going to drive to Dayton to pick up a load and just sit tight with it until the shutdown was over, but I was going to pick up that load first! Well, I started to pull my truck out of the yard. I was in my new Freightliner, and as I pull out onto the exit ramp I see that it's all blocked off by truckers and guys in cars. Three big guys, one holding a tire billy, come up to me and say, 'Buddy, we're all shutting down here. Just move that truck back where it was'. Well, I told them I was going to shut down, but I was going to do it in Dayton where I had a load waiting. They said, 'No, you're going to do it here'. I could see that one had a gun in his belt. I carry a can of mace with me, but, hell, I'm not going to get myself shot for not shutting down.

144

Knights of the road, 1958

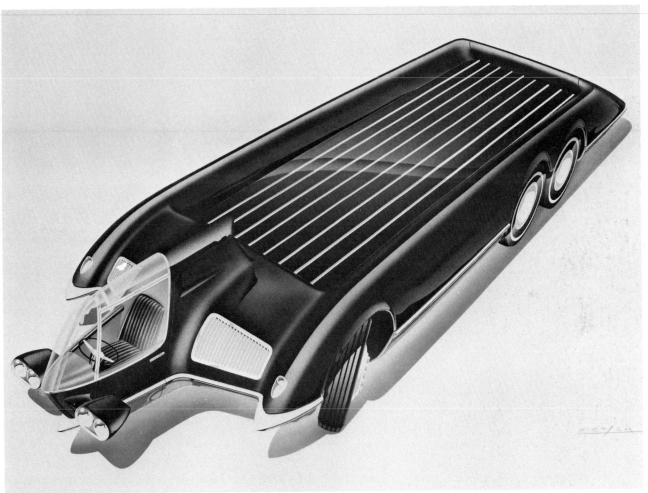

Truck of the future

"By this time I was plenty mad, so I told the guy with the billy that if he didn't let me through I would plow into his car with my truck. It was a standoff between him and me, and I finally laid on the hammer and took both doors of his Impala. He and the rest of them started yelling, getting pretty angry. Nobody tells me I can't drive my truck when I want, especially no other gearjammer. I made a quick turn and ran right over the flower beds and shrubs in front of the truck stop, pulled down a chain fence, and got out onto the highway. "I pulled into the truck stop at Dayton, and I could see an angry crowd waiting. The others had called ahead to tell them I was a scab. Man, I couldn't get off that highway. I lost the load, a bullet came through the windshield, the front of my truck was badly damaged, and you better damn well know that I couldn't ask a smokie for help that day. The next time a shutdown was called, there were enough guys like me around to not be interested. I guess the only good part of the shutdown I heard about were the good-looking broads that someone brought to the truck stop to try and convince us truckers to shut down. Whoever thought of that one sure had the right idea."

Group effort and organization has always best been handled by pencil-pushers rather than gearjammers. Truckers are used to making decisions for themselves—to go it alone or in a group, to wildcat or drive for a company, to be a teamster or an independent, to have a co-driver or roll alone—and each decision is likely to change the whole tone of his life.

At the inception of his career he must make his first important decision—how will he learn to drive a truck. The advertisements on TV, the ones offering free trucking dictionaries and bumper stickers, may tempt him to cough up the $900 for the course. In the hands of a bad school, the would-be driver will know as much about trucking when he graduates as he did when he registered. He might be able to circumnavigate a few pylons in an empty parking lot, and back up a ramp, but his lack of first-hand road knowledge makes him as dangerous to himself as he is to the other vehicles on the highway. Chances are he won't even get out of the parking lot, because he will be discovered as a novice by the employment office of the truck companies.

The best schools—the ones that turn out the top-notch professionals—are the schools operated by the big truck lines. They train drivers to drive company rigs and, to protect their investment, they expect the students to know the trucks from end to end in addition to being familiar with the rules of the road. Even

150

an experienced driver who signs up with a new company must complete a driving course, to relearn and revamp his driving skills.

For those who don't want to go to school—company-run or parking-lot variety—the best way to learn is to find a willing truckdriver and climb aboard. Many drivers can't remember exactly when they learned to drive. They probably had a father or an uncle who let them ride as a kid, and gradually taught them the intricacies of the shift pattern and clutch. The idea of a truck school seems as ludicrous to them as going to school to learn to breathe. Twenty years ago a man who went to school to learn truckdriving would have been laughed off the road. Truckdrivers were opposed to any educational system save the school of hard knocks. Trucking life couldn't be taught in a classroom any more than a cowboy could learn to rope cattle from a textbook. But like most of trucking, this, too, is changing. The image of the trucker is being reshaped and polished and modernized.

Sophie, Judy, and Inez are taking showers at a very modern truck stop in Connecticut. Like the men in the bathroom across the hall, their hard life is revealed in the blue-green fluorescent lights. The lines around their eyes seem deeply etched, and the redness of their short-nailed hands seems almost raw. All three women are truckdrivers.

Sophie, always ahead of her time, has been trucking for years. When she first started she would go for months without meeting another female trucker. She carried washcloths with her in her pocket to take sponge baths in the sinks of roadside ladies' rooms. She has been called everything from a "diesel dyke" to a "connivin' canary," and has had to toughen up to withstand the comments and freeze-outs she met from other truckers and annoyed waitresses. She used to especially enjoy the surprised looks from other truckers when she would jump out of the truck at the terminal, and she relished her own practiced skill with sixteen gears that she flaunted before suspicious eyes.

Judy and Inez have it better. They are the new breed of women truckers. Almost militant, and well aware of their rights to equal opportunity, they demand showers and bunks at the truck stops, and they expect courteous service from the waitresses. Inez has a child who lives with her ex-husband. She has a B.A. degree from a college in Pennsylvania, and owns her own rig, a white 1970 Reo. Last year she pulled in $18,000. "I hate the image of women truckers being 'butch' or trying to act like men just because they are in a job that draws mostly men. I do my job like a trucker and also a woman, and the two aren't opposites." Inez is wearing a navy blue worksuit with a cardigan sweater over it. She looks down at herself quickly. "You know, I like to look feminine when I drive. I guess 'feminine' isn't quite the word I want; more like well groomed. When I first started trucking, I wore cowboy boots and jeans and sometimes a leather jacket but I felt tough and almost like I was playing a bit in a play, trying to look like a trucker. I know you can't wear high heels and a frilly dress, but I found a pair of low heeled shoes that tie, and they do the job just fine."

Judy has stepped out of the shower and is getting dressed. She rolls her hair into a bun, and starts to anchor it with long pins. Ask Judy what she likes least about truckdriving and she doesn't hesitate to answer. "Well, I guess it's partly my fault, 'cause I have a flatbed trailer that needs all sorts of tarps and ropes to keep the load in place, but I hate the loading and unloading. I really got into trucking because I like to drive and see the country. The male drivers will tell you that the trouble with women truckers is that they are too weak, but just pull up at a terminal and they all stand around and watch, instead of helping like they do with each other. I weigh 150 pounds—that's as much as a lot of the wiry guys out here, but they see a woman unloading and they just stand around and gawk."

Neither of these women belongs to the National Women's Trucking Association. Founded by Jean Sawyer and operated from her sprawling seventeen-room house in Charleston, South Carolina, the NWTA works at promoting the image of the woman trucker. Jean Sawyer, herself a trucker, knew the problems that women met on the road, especially in truck stops designed for all-male clientele. Her first problem was to be acknowledged as a truckdriver, so she created a line of clothes for women, practical and simple, to be worn while driving. The clothes were embroidered with the NWTA emblem. Jean then hand-produced cards for the women to carry—their membership card in the organization, and ones with a space for a name bearing the slogan "You have been helped by a woman trucker"—presumably to hand to motorists or others in distress on the road. There are Day-Glow orange stickers to paste on your logbooks or notebooks—"The couple that trucks together stays together," and one for truck-stop rest rooms, "Please keep this rest room clean—another woman trucker will be here next." Jean Sawyer's organization also provides special insurance rates for its members, a newsletter

152

153

154

Jean Sawyer, president of the National Women's
Trucking Association

to help them find jobs, and a yearly convention with guest speakers from trucking lines and safety councils around the country.

The NWTA is unique, but it isn't the only truck association around that helps minority groups get a foot in a trucking career. The traditional image of the truckdriver has not only been male, but a white male with a red neck and a can of Blue Ribbon beer. While women drivers were regarded as amusing annoyances, black truckers were met with up-front hostility. Signs in southern truck stops telling the black trucker "Money spent here by black drivers will go to the K.K.K." do nothing for a black trucker's sense of southern hospitality.

Truck companies have always been reluctant to hire black drivers. They were afraid of co-driver problems and racial incidents at the terminals. The image that the truckdriver had patterned himself on—the cowboy, with his country-western music, his bouffanted blond woman, and his tightlipped camaraderie—had no room for the black man. This attitude stimulated the emergence of the Black Truckers Organization. Designed to show the black man or woman who wants to drive a truck where to begin and how to go about it, the organization, like the NWTA, acts as a clearing house for the problems of those who challenge traditions.

Despite the wide variations in feeling about women, blacks, teamsters, and where you can get the best breakfast, there is one thing that everybody agrees on—truckdriving is changing every day and the old ways are gone for good. Sometimes you can almost hear the death rattle in the old truckers' throats. The Interstate system has all but obliterated the small roads whose every curve sang of romance and danger. The little diner where the waitress remembered your name has given way to the sprawling cotton-bunned burger emporium. Even the things a driver talks about as he unwinds and coffees up at the truck stop are different.

Nowadays almost every long-haul truck on the road displays a three-foot silver antenna. It is hooked up to a Citizen's Band radio. The CB radio is perhaps the single most important factor that has changed the style of the trucker's life, pulling him by his ears into the 1970s. Trucking has always been a lonely occupation. It gave a man time to do a lot of thinking, and when he finally pulled into a diner or truck stop, he was eager for some good talking. He was anxious to hear about the latest gossip, the road conditions, the police activity, or where the action was; but mainly he wanted someone to share his thoughts with. This catharsis of talk after the long silence on the road swings the pendulum that has set the beat for the trucker's mythology and oral history. Instant friendship could be struck up against the flint of shared stories and gossip.

Now with a CB radio in each truck that spark is all but dead. Instead of long hours passed with nothing but the sounds of the road to soothe him, the trucker has a small squeaking box of a two-way radio to keep him company. By any standards the conversations are usually uninspired. They are mostly about the whereabouts of "smokie" or the road conditions up ahead. The hand and light signals once used extensively by truckers have drifted into oblivion, since this information can be relayed much faster and more accurately on the radio. The old-fashioned signals were not as cryptic as the non-trucker might expect. There were nine in all:

1 The hand is extended from the window palm up, and raised up and down to signify a weigh station up ahead.

2 A "V" sign is given with two fingers to indicate the presence of a hiding cop or radar up ahead.

3 Waving a logbook always means logbook check or some sort of official checkup ahead.

4 One blink of the lights is a greeting meaning "Hi."

5 Two blinks means trouble or an accident...slow down.

6 Three blinks means danger, I need help, or stop.

7 Tapping of the brake pedal to cause the rear lights to blink indicates to the truck behind that a cop is up ahead.

8 The index finger going in a circle then pointing ahead means the road is clear...let's make time.

9 The rolling of hands around each other means an accident or roll-over down the road.

After talking on the radio all day using only his CB handle, a trucker has dulled his appetite for companionship. When he pulls into the truck stop for the night, he is glad for the silence. If he does strike up a conversation, it might revolve around CB radios rather than the road danger of "smokie the bear in a plain brown wrapper" (the trooper in an unmarked car).

There are about six different truck shows a year, from the American Trucking Association's Truck Roadeo to the Wheeling, West Virginia, Trucker's Jamboree. Truckers from all over the country and Canada come to hear entertainers pay homage to them. Unfortunately, the trucker's income is often the raison d'etre for the festivities rather than any true love or appreciation for his way of life. The commercial expos bombard him with new products for his ego and his truck. The entertainment is heavy on the country-western side, and the Wheeling Jamboree features a round-up of trucker singing stars. Favorites like Red Sovine, Dave Dudley, and Dick Curless were the main attractions even over headliners like Buck Owens.

The show and exposition were supposedly "free" to truckers and their families, but the word "free" couldn't disguise the twenty-dollar taxi fare to the expo grounds, and the fact that performers worked in front of giant rear projection slides of new products. The expositions are crowded with new top-of-the-line trucks, chrome beauties that hold more attraction for the truckers than the entertainment. But even these are a source of disappointment. Advertised as available for test drives around the nearby race track, they are locked up the day of the show and available only for appreciation from afar. After having been chased away from the engine of a new Kenworth by an overzealous Jamboree guard, Robert, a trucker for 28 years, grumbled, "If I had just wanted to see the new trucks, I could have stayed home and read a magazine." He had come 1800 miles for the show, and was now standing in the pouring rain with one screaming child hanging from a pants leg, and an angry wife nearby complaining that Red Sovine didn't sing her request.

Not all expositions are set up to financially exploit the trucker. The American Trucking Association's Roadeo is geared towards promoting his image. The Roadeo is a test of driving skills open to interested truckers. Contestants are put through a competition based on their appearance, road logic, mechanical ability, personality, and skill at maneuvering around a tricky obstacle course. Like diesel-perfumed beauty contestants, the ATA Roadeo participants are often antagonized by the judges during the pre-trial interview to see if the driver's personality breaks under pressure. After the appearance of both the driver and his truck are judged, a written test covering all the rules of the road, first aid, and fire fighting is given. The written exam is the least popular part of the test. Then the drivers are given a truck with pre-arranged defects for them to uncover. There are eighty pieces of equipment they must examine and judge. Finally comes the field course, which is the heart of the examination. Although not as glamorous or as visually exciting as a real rodeo with Brahma-bull riding, the trucker's course requires a high degree of skill, involving the maneuvering of a truck with trailer or a double bottom rig through nar-

row passageways. Six victors are finally crowned and named "Champions of the Highway," each receiving a trophy and $1000.

The winners of the Truck Roadeo are the golden boys of trucking, and like any Jack Armstrong type, they are regarded with mixed emotions. Mrs. James Rosell, wife of a winner at the ATA Roadeo, says of her husband, "Jim won the doubles division. I guess that's the highest honor, since it's the hardest category. Jim loves trucking, but he does have time for our kids (one is adopted). He helps them take care of their registered cattle, and takes them to the 4-H Club. Jim is also a chief in the Naval Seabees, and has just gotten his license to lecture at truck training schools. He attends church regularly and doesn't believe it takes a dirty mouth to be a good driver."

"Bullshit! I'm as good a driver as any of those clowns." Three drivers are sitting in a booth at a local truck stop. They are not so enamored with the golden boys of the diesel world. Bring up the subject of the Roadeo, and you'll hear a long Bronx cheer. "I don't have to drive around in circles wearing a monkey suit to show I can drive. I'm too busy making money." His buddies laugh in approval.

Since its foundation the American Trucking Associations has been concerned with upgrading the trucker's image. Their public campaign likes to get 'em while they're young, providing first- and second-grade teachers with cardboard dolls of truckers and their rigs, looking clean and wholesome, and a list of professional services a trucker provides for the nation. The ATA tends to sweep under its bureaucratic rug the misfits, the pill heads, the womanizers, and the cowboys you can meet at any truck stop. Its vision is one of the trucker as small businessman, working hard for his money, and deserving respect for his labors. Of course, they are right. For too long the truckdriver has been mistakenly seen as a gypsy on eighteen wheels. He was a tough guy, a roughneck, too uncouth and uncivilized for the rest of society. He does work hard; his hours are brutal and long; and often he sacrifices his home and loved ones for his job. When he is unable to drive, he must depend on other drivers for help; and in more than one truck stop you'll see milk cartons and buckets placed on the counters with little signs asking for donations for some poor busted-up trucker.

The life at its worst can be demeaning and unrewarding, but at its best, it makes a nine-to-five alternative look like a prison camp. A man can't be free if he is too carefully insulated and too well protected, because along with the benefits of protection come the strings

**Dave Dudley performs, Truckers' Jamboree
Wheeling, West Virginia**

159

that tie you down, and the rules and regulations that keep you in somebody else's line. But the times are too complex for the last American cowboy to stay on the road without help. As he glides down a six-lane highway instead of a back road, or sleeps in a Holiday Inn instead of a bunkhouse, or finds a mechanic every mile to fix his truck, the quality of his life changes. Each night he can tune his radio to the Charlie Douglas Road Gang Show or the Buddy Ray Trucker Show and hear the music and news that is programmed exclusively for him. He can talk on his CB radio whenever he feels lonely, and he doesn't even have to search for the wanton women, since they are right there on Channel 10 broadcasting to him. On Thursday night he can watch "Movin' On," or a rerun of "Duel" or "Tandem," or go out to see "Truck Stop Women" or "Moonfire," the latter produced by *Overdrive* Magazine and starring their own good-will ambassador, Chuck Napier. A trucker might be flattered by all the attention, but he will surely be horrified to learn of Commander Cody, singing rock 'n' roll truck songs to audiences of glittering unisexual kids. And maybe the guy in the truck next to him will turn out to be a woman, or a black, or a kid with hair down to his shoulders. The last American cowboy is becoming the American Cowperson, and even his trusted CB radio is evaporating his myths and stories. The six-cylinder horse is being replaced by an office on wheels.

The future of truckdriving will not be found in the trucker TV shows, or reflected in the organizations shaping drivers to fit their own special, tailored image, or even in militant magazines. Look to the men and women who drive, men like Country Jack: "There ain't no future in truckdrivin', that's just the point, there ain't no future, and there ain't no past; there's just now, and now is moving, and seeing sights and faces and new things to do. Truckdriving is doin' what you want when you want. I don't ever want to get off this road, just continue on it 'till the day I die, and then they can bury me on the side of the road for all I care, 'cause I will have done it all anyway, just the way I wanted to."

Jean Sawyer

Jean Sawyer keeps her collection of blond wigs in a plastic laundry basket. She owns over 150, all different lengths and styles picked up in discount stores around Charleston, South Carolina. Under the wigs, there is a yard of her own auburn hair rolled into a flat bun and concealed from the eyes of the world. Jean Sawyer started wearing wigs when she started driving trucks, never dreaming that either would become a consuming passion.

Jean is not just another woman truckdriver. She is the president of the National Woman's Trucking Association, an organization she founded four years ago. The headquarters of the NWTA is her sprawling and ramshackle seventeen-room home on the outskirts of Charleston.

The first thing one notices from the winding driveway are the cars scattered about on the lawn, including two red Cadillacs bearing the license plates "Victim I" and "Victim II" and an El Camino pickup truck with "NWTA" on its bumper. The Cadillacs are vintage years—1959 and 1961, with huge red sharkfins and chromed mammaries thrusting forward. Jean's favorite color is red, and even her Kenworth cabover attests to this preference.

Jean Sawyer, driving either her Cadillac or her truck, dressed in a red jumpsuit and crowned with her blond glamour wig and harlequin glasses is a sure-fire traffic stopper. She is a tiny woman, pure nerve and honed down to the bone with the help of her "energy pills." Her cheeks are hollowed and her intense, birdlike eyes follow the slightest movement. She is constantly in motion but seems to be a frame out of sync, a time-motion study gone haywire, always moving but never quite getting there. She didn't always plan to be a truckdriver. But planning has little to do with her life. Her "Victim" license plates are no joke to her. Life hasn't treated her gently and she learned to live by her wits.

She has three children; the oldest at fifteen is an alumnus of a southern detention home and the two youngest seem to be headed for a similar future. Their high spirits ride roughshod over everything in their paths. Jean will tell you that out of desperation she pretended to have died one day while vacuum cleaning in order to get the attention of her sons who were tearing around the house with razor blades scraping at decals that they had pasted on the windows. The boys stopped for a moment when they saw her still body lying motionless next to the Hoover but then leaped right over her into the kitchen for a double handful of cookies.

The husbands that Jean Sawyer has collected include a legless con artist from Las Vegas who schooled her in getting what she needed. She has served time in a Tallahassee jail where acid was poured on her crotch by inmates when she complained about them to the matron. She chronicled her stay in jail on a roll of toilet paper. Written in her tiny handwriting it tells of the liquor smuggled in shampoo bottles, the lesbianism, the brutality, and the corruption. The jail term was the result of eight hundred dollars in bad checks written on a journey cross country with her children in an effort to find their father. Even on the lam, Jean traveled first class, and she checked out of a Holiday Inn when her boys reported spotting a "nigger" in the swimming pool.

A sense of irony surrounds Jean Sawyer. She arrives at the welfare office in an autumn haze mink coat. She roars into a truck stop in the flashiest truck around. She takes a *Wall Street Journal* reporter on a truck ride so hair-raising he begs to be let off at the first opportunity. She loves to give the finger to the world, but feels victimized by its reaction.

She has been called "Hell on Wheels" by her male cohorts, yet she is at once naive and righteous. She won't drink liquor or even keep it in the house. Her minister is her good friend and she is generous with her time and money to the church. The seventeen-room house serves as a home for wayward girls, and between fights with her own social worker and visiting her kids in detention homes, she tries to help others. She takes in teenagers in trouble, and treats them well.

Living by her wits, fortified by the love of her truck-driving boyfriend and the gifts from her "sugar daddy," she feeds her strays porterhouse steaks and gives them new clothes and affection. Her neighbors don't approve of her life. They don't like the cars on the lawn or the chickens out back. The sanitation department is always fining her for the condition of her property. The inside of the house is equally eclectic. The headboard on her king-size bed is a velvet heart. The living room is littered with dead animal skulls and mummified alligator heads wearing motorcycle hats. There are scores of photographs—neo-Johnny Stompanato boyfriends, airbrushed pictures of Jean in her autumn haze mink stole, and pictures from the war showing her as the USO cover girl of the week.

Her closets overflow with clothes bought at Goodwill and thrift shops around town. Off the road Jean becomes a back-page fashion plate with her brocade dresses and mod vinyl ponchos. Her southern roots

demand femininity and, whether as a truckdriver or motorcyclist, she is always dressed befitting a queen of the road. She is unimpressed by feminism, preferring to use her "womanly wiles," but she admits a debt of gratitude to NOW for getting her the only good lawyer she ever had, and she's had quite a few. What Jean Sawyer can't get lawyers to fix for her, she takes care of herself. With her small printing press in the basement, she creates stationery with legal letterheads ranging from bogus law firms to the "Palmetto Security Agency." She is prepared to take on the world. She carries a silver private investigator's badge in her wallet, and lines her walls with mail-order diplomas to help her through the obstacle course her life has become.

One dependable solution Jean has found for her problems is to take to the highways, and make a living while staying two steps ahead of the wreckage she has left behind. Her lust for the open road and the escape it offers has set a pattern for her life. The thrill of the gears meshing and the black smoke blowing from her Kenworth's stacks are as old as truckdriving and as new as a platinum-wigged Rebel queen pushing sixteen gears.

Jean Sawyer at home

Jane

She's never hooked a glad hand
To complete the flow of air,
She's never slid the tandems
To distribute the weight up there.

She's never clutched that mighty rig
Nor turned that giant wheel,
She's never slept in a sleeper cab
And probably never will.

Still she's as much a trucker
As any on the road,
For she's diesel fuel in her veins
And smoke blowin' cross her soul.

Jack Hamilton,
Truckdriver